hamlyn

Sauce

Joanna Farrow

Note

Both metric and imperial measurements have been given in all recipes.
Use one set of measurements only, and not a mixture of both.

Standard level spoon measurements are used in all recipes.
1 tablespoon = one 15 ml spoon
1 teaspoon = one 5 ml spoon

The Department of Health advises that eggs should not be consumed raw.
This book contains dishes made with raw or lightly cooked eggs. It is
prudent for vulnerable people such as pregnant and nursing mothers,
invalids, the elderly, babies and young children to avoid uncooked or lightly
cooked dishes made with eggs. Once prepared, these dishes should be kept
refrigerated and used promptly.

This book includes dishes made with nuts and nut derivatives. It is advisable
for customers with known allergic reactions to nuts and nut derivatives and
those who may be potentially vulnerable to these allergies, such as pregnant
and nursing mothers, invalids, the elderly, babies and children to avoid
dishes made with nuts and nut oils. It is also prudent to check the labels of
pre-prepared ingredients for the possible inclusion of nut derivatives.

Ovens should be pre-heated to the specified temperature – if using a fan-
assisted oven, follow the manufacturer's instructions for adjusting the time
and the temperature.

Vegetarians should look for the 'V' symbol on a cheese to ensure it is made
with vegetarian rennet. There are vegetarian forms of Parmesan, feta,
Cheddar, Cheshire, Red Leicester, dolcelatte and many goats' cheeses.

First published in Great Britain in 2004 by Hamlyn,
a division of Octopus Publishing Group Ltd
2–4 Heron Quays, London E14 4JP

Copyright © Octopus Publishing Group Ltd 2004

ISBN 0 600 60950 2

A CIP catalogue record for this book is available
from the British Library.

Printed and bound in China

10 9 8 7 6 5 4 3 2 1

contents

Introduction

A good sauce can transform the most simply cooked piece of meat, chicken, fish or even a selection of vegetables into a lively and interesting dish. The sauce complements and enhances the food it accompanies, adding flavour, colour, texture and moisture without overpowering or detracting from it.

This book is intended as an essential guide to sauce-making. It's divided into 'true classics', the sauces we all know about but don't necessarily know how to make, followed by a range of recipes, some traditional and others modern and innovative. Most of the recipes are surprisingly quick and easy to make and need very few ingredients, so the results will always be rewarding as long as you choose good quality raw materials. To make menu planning easier, the recipes offer 'Great with' ideas. These should be used as a guide, rather than a hard and fast rule; you may well have other preferences for the focus of the meal.

Essential ingredients

Stock Any sauce that uses meat, fish or vegetable stock will taste better if you use a homemade stock. Don't be put off by this, stocks are easy to make, cost very little and it's not difficult to get into the habit of making them. Use the leftover bones from a roast or ask your butcher for bones when you're in the shop, or use a selection of fresh vegetables when they pile up in the refrigerator. If you don't need the stock for a few days, freeze it for a ready supply. Cartons or tubs of ready-made stock make a good alternative but are expensive for the amount you get. Concentrated liquid stocks are an adequate standby, as are good quality cubes and powders. These are often quite salty, though, and should therefore be used sparingly.

Butter Always use unsalted butter for sauce-making, although you can use lightly salted butter if you run out. Salted butter has a less creamy flavour and is more likely to burn.

Oils You don't need a huge supply of oils in the storecupboard. A richly flavoured, extra virgin olive oil is ideal for many Mediterranean-style sauces, while a light olive oil is more suitable for a sauce where you need a good oil but don't want its flavour to dominate, for example in mayonnaise. Choose a mildly flavoured oil such as sunflower or groundnut oil for other recipes including Indian and Asian-style sauces. A little sesame oil adds a delicious flavour to Asian dishes although it cannot be used for frying because of its low smoking point. Nut oils such as walnut and hazelnut are particularly good in recipes where you want to emphasize a nutty flavour.

Herbs Fresh herbs have a far better flavour than dried ones but are best used as soon as possible after buying or picking.

Delicate herbs deteriorate after several days in the refrigerator.

Eggs Use really fresh eggs in sauces, preferably free-range organic ones. This is particularly important in a recipe such as Crème Anglaise where the eggs provide the colour and flavour.

Cream An essential ingredient, cream is often used to add a velvety-smooth finishing touch to a sauce. Provided it's really fresh, neither double nor single cream should separate even when it's boiled unless it's mixed with a high proportion of acidic ingredients. Crème fraîche, which makes a good alternative when you want a tangier, but still creamy flavour, is best not cooked at high temperatures.

Equipment *Very little specialist equipment is needed to make a good sauce and most well-equipped kitchens will already contain the essentials. Decent pots and pans are vital and it's worth shopping around if you're thinking of buying more. A food processor or blender will save you no end of time and trouble.*

Pots and pans A set of three or four saucepans is all you need. Always use a heavy-based pan for sauce-making (and most other types of cooking) as it will conduct heat more efficiently, and a sauce will be far less likely to burn if left to cook for a while. Most pans come with lids, although in some cases these are sold separately. Generally, lids are only used for simmering when you don't want any liquid to evaporate. Some pans have a capacity gauge on the inside. This is useful if you're reducing a stock or sauce by a certain amount. A large pan – 5–6 litres (8½–10 pints) – is most suitable for making stocks as there is plenty of room for the liquid to bubble up without the risk of it boiling over. A medium pan – about 2 litres (3½ pints) – can be used for making most sauces and can also serve as a bain marie, partly filled with boiling water, with a heatproof bowl resting over it for making delicate sauces. A small pan is best for sugar syrups, and for cooking or reheating small quantities of sauce.

All pans come in a choice of materials. Copper pans are perfect for sauce-making as they are such good conductors of heat, but they tend to be very expensive. Stainless steel pans are the most popular choice. Lightweight and easy to clean, they're available in a wide range of styles. The best stainless steel pans have a steel-enclosed aluminium base for good heat conduction. Aluminium pans also conduct heat well but should not be used for cooking fruit and acidic ingredients which readily react with the metal. A large heavy-based frying pan is useful for frying vegetables and meat, particularly when you want the ingredients to brown.

Spoons and whisks Wooden spoons are used for stirring and thickening sauces, although many cooks prefer to use a balloon or coiled whisk for thickening as they are more efficient at removing any lumps. Keep an assortment of different-sized whisks but avoid very large ones that are less effective and more likely to fall out of the pan. A slotted metal spoon is good for draining ingredients after frying, or skimming the fat or froth that accumulates on the surface of a stock. A large metal ladle is useful for transferring liquids and a rubber spatula effectively scrapes out thick sauces like Mayonnaise or Hollandaise without any wastage.

Sieves and strainers Conical strainers are good for sauce-making as the liquid strains through the base rather than splashing all over the work surface.

A conical strainer with small holes is useful for straining stocks while a wire mesh sieve is good for squeezing out juices from fruit or vegetable pulps and giving a velvety smooth consistency. For straining large quantities of meat or fish stock, you can place an ordinary colander with handles over a large glass bowl so you have both hands free to tip the stock from the saucepan into the colander.

Other equipment A food processor or blender takes an awful lot of the effort out of chopping vegetables, mixing pastes and puréeing cooked ingredients. A small food processor, or a larger one with a small inner bowl, is ideal for spice blends and small quantities of herbs, nuts, etc. A hand-held electric immersion blender is great for blending and puréeing a sauce while still in the saucepan, although you can't guarantee a perfectly smooth result with this method. For making some of the more rustic sauces in a traditional way, use a large, sturdy pestle and mortar.

Techniques

Thickening sauces There are various ways of thickening a sauce; sometimes it is the first step of a recipe, as in a roux, in other cases it's a finishing step and uses ingredients such as egg yolks, cream and butter. The most important rule is to avoid over-thickening. A sauce made cloyingly thick with flour or cornflour is unpalatable and can ruin a whole dish. As a general guide, most sauces are sufficiently thickened when they thinly coat the back of a wooden spoon. Let the sauce cool slightly on the spoon, then run your finger along it – it should leave a clear impression.

Roux A blend of butter and flour, lightly cooked together before the liquid is added, as in a Béchamel Sauce (see page 16). If the roux is cooked a little more it forms the base of a Velouté Sauce (see page 80), or cooked further still, it's used for brown sauces (see page 30).

Beurre manié This is also a mixture of butter and flour, but here they are kneaded together in a bowl to make a paste and then whisked into the cooked sauce until it thickens. It is a useful method for thickening a disappointingly thin sauce, or a stew or casserole in which the juice is very thin. Use about 15 g (½ oz) each of softened butter and plain flour to 600 ml (1 pint) of liquid.

Cornflour Cornflour must be blended with a little water, stock or juice before it is added to a sauce. It's rarely used in traditional sauces but sometimes crops up in Asian-style ones.

Egg yolks and cream These are good for adding extra flavour and richness to a thin sauce, particularly those with a stock base. Blend 2 egg yolks with 150 ml (¼ pint) of single cream and add a ladleful of the hot but not boiling sauce. Tip the

mixture into the pan and cook over a very gentle heat, whisking or stirring until it is slightly thickened.

Enriching with butter Whisking a little chilled butter into a finished sauce thickens it slightly and gives it a lighter flavour and glossier finish.

Reducing Provided it doesn't include ingredients like eggs or yogurt, or any ingredients that are likely to curdle, a thin stock or sauce can be reduced and thickened by rapid boiling. If you are reducing a stock, don't start boiling it until you have removed the bones, etc. The reducing time will vary depending on the amount of liquid, so keep an eye on the pan. If necessary skim off any froth on the surface and don't season the sauce until you have reduced it.

Puréeing Some sauces, particularly fruit or vegetable ones, can be thickened by blending the ingredients, either in a food processor or blender, or using an immersion blender.

Making a bouquet garni Tying a mixture of herbs in a bouquet garni means you can easily remove it from the sauce after cooking. A classic bouquet garni includes bay leaves, sprigs of thyme and parsley stalks which can be wrapped in a length of celery or leek and tied with string.

Skinning tomatoes Put the tomatoes into a bowl, cover with boiling water and leave until the skins split. This will take about 1–2 minutes. Spear one tomato with a sharp knife and check that the skin peels off easily before draining them all.

Saving a lumpy sauce Use a balloon whisk to vigorously beat the sauce, or place in a food processor or blender and blend for 1 minute until smooth.

Beef stock

When you buy a piece of beef, get the bones as well and ask the butcher to cut them into manageable pieces. Cheap cuts of beef and trimmings can be used instead of bones but this tends to be more expensive. For a dark, richly coloured stock, roast the bones in a preheated oven, 200°C (400°F), Gas Mark 6, for 45 minutes beforehand.

PREPARATION TIME: 10 minutes
COOKING TIME: 3 hours
MAKES: about 1 litre (1¾ pints)

750 g (1½ lb) beef bones
1 large onion, unpeeled and quartered
1 large carrot, roughly chopped
2 celery sticks, roughly chopped
1 bouquet garni
1 teaspoon black peppercorns
1.8 litres (3 pints) cold water

1 Put the bones into a large heavy-based saucepan with the onion, carrot, celery, bouquet garni and peppercorns. Add the cold water and bring slowly to the boil.

2 Reduce the heat and simmer the stock very gently for 3 hours, skimming the surface from time to time if necessary.

3 Strain the stock through a large sieve, preferably a conical one, and leave to cool. Don't squeeze the juice out of the vegetables or the stock will be cloudy.

4 Leave the stock to cool completely, then chill. Remove any layer of fat that might have set on the surface before use.

Variation: Lamb stock is less versatile than beef and chicken stock because of its distinctive flavour. If you have plenty of bones, though, it's well worth making some for lamb dishes. Roast the bones first, then follow the recipe for beef stock, simmering the stock for just 1½ hours.

Beef stock

Great with: *pork and lamb chops, duck breasts and venison, or for stirring into casseroles or gravies*

Chicken stock

Ideally chicken stock is made using a raw carcass, either from the butcher or from a chicken you've jointed for a recipe. However, don't throw away a cooked carcass from a Sunday roast; it makes a very acceptable, well-flavoured stock that might just be a little cloudy.

PREPARATION TIME: 10 minutes

COOKING TIME: 1½ hours

MAKES: about 1 litre (1¾ pints)

1 large chicken carcass, plus any trimmings

giblets, except the liver, if available

1 onion, quartered

1 celery stick, roughly chopped

1 bouquet garni, or 3 bay leaves

1 teaspoon black peppercorns

1.8 litres (3 pints) cold water

1 Put the chicken carcass, giblets, onion, celery, bouquet garni and peppercorns into a large heavy-based saucepan and add the cold water.

2 Make the stock following the recipe for Beef Stock (see page 10), but simmer it for just 1½ hours.

Vegetable stock

You can use almost any mixture of vegetables, but they must be really fresh. Make sure you include some onion, but omit vegetables with strong flavours such as cabbage and starchy ones like potatoes which will make the stock cloudy. For a dark stock, leave the skins on the onions and use plenty of mushrooms.

PREPARATION TIME: 10 minutes

COOKING TIME: 45 minutes

MAKES: about 1 litre (1¾ pints)

1 tablespoon sunflower oil

2 onions, roughly chopped

2 carrots, roughly chopped

2 celery sticks, roughly chopped

500 g (1 lb) mixture other vegetables, such as parsnips, fennel, leeks, courgettes, mushrooms and tomatoes

1 bouquet garni

1 teaspoon black peppercorns

1.5 litres (2½ pints) cold water

1 Heat the oil in a large heavy-based saucepan and gently fry all the vegetables for 5 minutes.

2 Add the cold water, then follow the method for Beef Stock (see page 10), simmering the stock for just 40 minutes.

Fish stock

Don't use oily fish in a stock – it will make it greasy and give it an overpoweringly strong flavour. Fish stock needs much less cooking than meat stocks so take care not to overcook it or its flavour will deteriorate.

PREPARATION TIME: 5 minutes

COOKING TIME: 25 minutes

MAKES: about 1 litre (1¾ pints)

25 g (1 oz) butter

3 shallots, roughly chopped

1 small leek, roughly chopped

1 celery stick or piece of fennel, roughly chopped

1 kg (2 lb) white fish or shellfish bones, heads and trimmings

150 ml (¼ pint) dry white wine

several parsley stalks

½ lemon, sliced

1 teaspoon black or white peppercorns

1 litre (1¾ pints) cold water

1 Melt the butter in a large heavy-based saucepan until bubbling. Add all the vegetables and fry gently for 5 minutes to soften them slightly, without browning.

2 Add the fish bones, wine, parsley, lemon slices, peppercorns and cold water.

3 Follow the method for Beef Stock (see page 10), simmering the stock for just 20 minutes.

Keeping stock

Meat and chicken stock will keep in the refrigerator for up to 4 days. Vegetable stock can be stored for up to 2 days. Fish stock should be used within 24 hours. If you want to keep stock longer, freeze it in small containers.

These are the recipes that date back to the days when sauces formed the foundation of classic cooking – recipes such as Béchamel Sauce which, although interesting enough to serve as it is, tends to be used as a base for numerous variations. Hollandaise Sauce is perhaps one of the most delicious sauces of all. Velvety smooth and delicate, nothing beats its luxuriant quality, served smothering freshly steamed asparagus or chunky pieces of fish. Despite the availability of some well-made bought mayonnaises, any cook, whether beginner or advanced, will feel a real sense of achievement on making it from scratch. Finally there are the deep, rich brown sauces, the sort that are now frequently displaced by lighter, more modern flavours, but are still held in high esteem as true classics.

Béchamel sauce

This sauce features in so many dishes that it's worth getting it just right. It can be spooned over vegetables, gratin style, layered in baked dishes like lasagne, or tossed with pasta, and with extra flavourings, it can be transformed into different sauces. This quantity makes enough for four servings as an accompaniment.

PREPARATION TIME: 10 minutes, plus infusing
COOKING TIME: 10 minutes
SERVES: 4

300 ml (½ pint) full cream milk
½ small onion
1 bay leaf
½ teaspoon peppercorns
3–4 parsley stalks
15 g (½ oz) butter
15 g (½ oz) plain flour
freshly grated nutmeg
salt and pepper

1 Put the milk into a saucepan with the onion, bay leaf, peppercorns and parsley stalks, and bring almost to the boil. Remove the pan from the heat and leave to infuse for 20 minutes. Strain the milk through a sieve into a jug.

2 Melt the butter in a heavy-based saucepan until bubbling. Tip in the flour and stir quickly to combine. Cook the mixture gently, stirring constantly with a wooden spoon, for 1–2 minutes to make a smooth, pale roux.

3 Remove the pan from the heat and gradually whisk in the warm milk, stirring constantly until the sauce is completely smooth. Return the pan to a moderate heat and cook, stirring, until the sauce comes to the boil.

4 Reduce the heat to low and continue to cook the sauce for about 5 minutes, stirring frequently until it is smooth and glossy and thinly coats the back of the spoon. Season to taste with salt, pepper and plenty of freshly grated nutmeg.

Variation:

Rich cheese sauce *This smooth and creamy*
cheese sauce is both simple and delicious, and ideal for using up
leftover cheese. This recipe uses a mixture of Cheddar and Parmesan
but you can use small pieces of Gruyère or Stilton, or combine
several different cheeses.

PREPARATION TIME: 10 minutes

COOKING TIME: 10 minutes

SERVES: 4

300 ml (½ pint) full cream milk

½ small onion

1 bay leaf

15 g (½ oz) butter

15 g (½ oz) plain flour

**1 teaspoon green peppercorns in brine,
  rinsed and drained**

75 g (3 oz) mature Cheddar cheese, grated

15 g (½ oz) freshly grated Parmesan cheese

freshly grated nutmeg

salt

1 Follow steps 1, 2 and 3 of Béchamel Sauce (see left), omitting the black peppercorns and parsley.

2 Using a pestle and mortar, lightly crush the green peppercorns until they are broken into small pieces. Add them to the sauce with the cheeses and a little nutmeg. Cook over a gentle heat, stirring frequently, for about 5 minutes until smooth and glossy. Check the seasoning and serve hot.

Coconut and coriander sauce

Although this recipe uses the basic white sauce method, coconut milk gives it a flavour that's best matched with Asian ingredients such as coriander and lime. It is really good with grilled chicken and fish.

PREPARATION TIME: 10 minutes, plus infusing

COOKING TIME: 10 minutes

SERVES: 4

400 ml (14 fl oz) can coconut milk

25 g (1 oz) piece fresh root ginger, grated

2 bay leaves

15 g (½ oz) butter

2 tablespoons plain flour

finely grated rind and juice of 1 lime

7 g (¼ oz) coriander leaves, chopped

2 teaspoons caster sugar

salt and pepper

1 Put the coconut milk into a small saucepan with the ginger and bay leaves and bring almost to the boil. Remove from the heat and leave to infuse for 20 minutes. Strain the coconut milk through a sieve into a jug.

2 Follow steps 2 and 3 of Béchamel Sauce on page 16.

3 Add the lime rind and juice, coriander, sugar and a little salt and pepper. Cook very gently for 3–5 minutes until the sauce is slightly thickened and smooth.

Creamy sorrel sauce *Shredded into a creamy white sauce, sorrel gives a fresh lemony tang that goes beautifully with lamb, chicken or fish dishes.*

PREPARATION TIME: 10 minutes

COOKING TIME: 12 minutes

SERVES: 4

75 g (3 oz) sorrel

40 g (1½ oz) butter

2 shallots, finely chopped

2 tablespoons plain flour

150 ml (¼ pint) dry white wine

150 ml (¼ pint) single cream

freshly grated nutmeg

salt and pepper

1 Discard the stalks from the sorrel and finely shred the leaves. Melt 15 g (½ oz) of the butter in a heavy-based saucepan and fry the shallots for 3 minutes until softened. Add the sorrel and fry for a further 2 minutes until wilted.

2 Melt the remaining butter in a separate pan until bubbling. Tip in the flour and cook gently, stirring constantly with a wooden spoon, for 2 minutes.

3 Remove the pan from the heat and gradually whisk in the wine, then the cream. Bring to the boil, then reduce the heat and add the sorrel and shallot mixture. Cook gently for about 5 minutes until the sauce is smooth and glossy and thinly coats the back of the spoon. Sprinkle with nutmeg and season with salt and pepper to taste.

Wild mushroom sauce

Dried wild mushrooms have an intensely strong flavour and a handful will really boost the flavour of ordinary mushrooms in a sauce. Use any type of dried mushrooms or a mixed bag, whichever is available.

PREPARATION TIME: 10 minutes, plus soaking

COOKING TIME: 12 minutes

SERVES: 5–6

15 g (½ oz) dried mushrooms

150 ml (¼ pint) boiling water

25 g (1 oz) butter

150 g (5 oz) chestnut mushrooms, chopped

15 g (½ oz) plain flour

150 ml (¼ pint) full cream milk

2 tablespoons Madeira or sherry

3 tablespoons double cream

salt and pepper

1 Put the dried mushrooms into a small bowl and cover with the boiling water. Leave to soak for 15 minutes.

2 Melt half the butter in a heavy-based saucepan until bubbling and fry the chestnut mushrooms for 5 minutes. Add the remaining butter. When it has melted, stir in the flour and cook, stirring, for 2 minutes.

3 Put the dried mushrooms and their soaking liquid in a food processor or blender and whizz until the mushrooms are finely chopped. Gradually blend the mushrooms and liquid, then the milk into the pan.

4 Return to the heat and bring to the boil then reduce the heat and cook gently for 3–4 minutes until the sauce thinly coats the back of a wooden spoon. Stir in the Madeira or sherry, cream and a little salt and pepper. Heat through for 1 minute.

Soubise sauce *This classic French recipe combines tender, sautéed onions with cream, nutmeg and Béchamel Sauce and goes very well with roast chicken, goose, guinea fowl or veal chops. It can be served as it is, or if you want a thoroughly smooth sauce, whizz it in a food processor and then reheat it to serve.*

PREPARATION TIME: 10 minutes

COOKING TIME: 10 minutes

SERVES : 5–6

25 g (1 oz) butter

2 large onions, finely chopped

1 quantity Béchamel Sauce (see page 16)

100 ml (3½ fl oz) double cream

freshly grated nutmeg

salt and pepper

1 Melt the butter in a heavy-based saucepan until bubbling. Add the onions and fry over a very gentle heat for about 6–8 minutes until they are very soft but not browned.

2 Add the Béchamel sauce and cream to the pan and grate plenty of nutmeg into the sauce. Reheat gently for 2 minutes and season with salt and pepper to taste.

Parsley sauce

Traditional sauces like this one are often shunned in favour of those with more complex or exotic ingredients, but a well-made parsley sauce can be just as good, so long as you use really fresh, fragrant parsley. If serving this with boiled ham you can use the poaching juices from the meat for a stock, providing it is not too salty.

PREPARATION TIME: 10 minutes

COOKING TIME: 5 minutes

SERVES : 4

15 g (½ oz) curly parsley

250 ml (8 fl oz) **Fish Stock** (see page 13) or ham stock

25 g (1 oz) butter

25 g (1 oz) plain flour

250 ml (8 fl oz) milk

3 tablespoons single cream

salt and pepper

1 Discard any tough stalks from the parsley and put it into a food processor or blender with half the stock. Blend until the parsley is very finely chopped.

2 Melt the butter in a heavy-based saucepan until bubbling. Tip in the flour and stir quickly to combine. Cook the mixture gently, stirring constantly with a wooden spoon, for 2 minutes.

3 Remove the pan from the heat and gradually whisk in the parsley-flavoured stock, then the remaining stock, until smooth. Whisk in the milk. Return to the heat and bring to the boil, stirring. Reduce the heat and continue to cook the sauce for about 5 minutes, stirring frequently, until it is smooth and glossy. The sauce should thinly coat the back of the spoon.

4 Stir in the cream and a little salt and pepper (remembering that if you've used ham stock, it might be quite salty) and heat gently to warm through.

Parsley sauce

Great with: *poached or grilled cod or haddock, smoked white fish and gammon steaks*

Mayonnaise

Mayonnaise is the most versatile chilled sauce. It is delicious as it is, or it can be used as a base for many fabulous variations. Make it with sunflower or light olive oil but avoid very strong olive oils as their flavour can be too overpowering. Good quality egg yolks, preferably organic ones, will also give the best results.

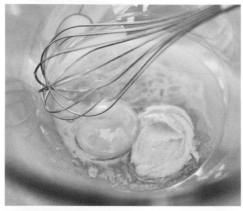

PREPARATION TIME: 10 minutes
SERVES: 6–8

2 egg yolks
2 teaspoons Dijon mustard
1–2 tablespoons white wine vinegar
250 ml (8 fl oz) oil
salt and pepper

1 Put the egg yolks, mustard, 1 tablespoon of the vinegar and a little salt and pepper in a large bowl and whisk lightly with a balloon whisk to combine.

2 Whisking continuously, start adding the oil, a few drops at a time, until the sauce starts to thicken.

3 Gradually add the remaining oil in a very thin, steady stream until the mayonnaise is thick and glossy. Don't add the oil too quickly or the mayonnaise might start to separate. If this happens, try whisking in 1 tablespoon warm water. If the mixture curdles completely, whisk another egg yolk in a separate bowl and gradually whisk it into the curdled sauce.

4 Check the seasoning, adding a little more vinegar if the sauce tastes bland. Mayonnaise can be kept, covered, in the refrigerator for up to 2 days.

Shortcut mayonnaise: Blend the egg yolks, mustard, vinegar and salt and pepper in a food processor or blender. With the machine running, very slowly pour in the oil, starting with a few drops until the sauce thickens, then pouring in a thin, steady stream. Season as above.

Variation:

Aïoli

Aïoli is a mayonnaise generously flavoured with garlic. Only use really fresh, juicy garlic, or, for a change, try smoked garlic. Serve aïoli with Mediterranean fish soups (as an accompaniment with toasted croûtons), salt cod, roasted vegetables and as a dip for chips or crudités. It will keep for 2 days tightly covered in the refrigerator.

PREPARATION TIME: 10 minutes

SERVES: 6–8

2 egg yolks

1 teaspoon Dijon mustard

1–2 tablespoons lemon juice

2 garlic cloves, crushed

good pinch of cayenne pepper

250 ml (8 fl oz) sunflower or light olive oil

salt

1 Put the egg yolks, mustard, 1 tablespoon of the lemon juice, the garlic, cayenne pepper and a little oil in a large mixing bowl and whisk together lightly to combine.

2 Follow steps 2, 3 and 4 of the Mayonnaise recipe (see opposite). Cover and chill until ready to serve.

Sauce verte

Plenty of parsley, tarragon and spinach leaves give this herb mayonnaise its lovely emerald colour. The mayonnaise can be made a couple of days in advance but add the herbs on the day you serve it, so they retain their fresh flavour.

PREPARATION TIME: 5 minutes

SERVES: 6–8

25 g (1 oz) flat leaf parsley

15 g (½ oz) tarragon

50 g (2 oz) baby spinach leaves

2 spring onions, trimmed and roughly chopped

1 quantity Mayonnaise (see page 22)

salt and pepper

1 Discard any tough stalks from the parsley, tarragon and spinach. Put the leaves and spring onions in a food processor or blender and blend until chopped to a thick paste, scraping down the mixture from the sides of the bowl if necessary.

2 Add 3 tablespoons of the mayonnaise to the paste and blend thoroughly until combined. Add the remaining mayonnaise and blend very lightly until the ingredients are evenly combined. Check the seasoning and turn the sauce into a small serving dish.

Tartare and green peppercorn sauce

Crushed green peppercorns give the classic ingredients of Tartare Sauce a tangy lift. It's great with any white fish, particularly fish and chips and keeps well in the refrigerator for two to three days.

PREPARATION TIME: 12 minutes

SERVES: 5–8

1 quantity Mayonnaise (see page 22)

2 tablespoons chopped parsley or chervil

4 small gherkins, finely chopped

1 tablespoon capers, rinsed, drained and chopped

6 pitted green olives, finely chopped

2 teaspoons green peppercorns in brine, rinsed and lightly crushed

salt

1 Put the mayonnaise into a bowl and add the remaining ingredients. Beat well to combine and season with a little salt if needed. Cover and chill until ready to serve.

Seafood sauce
A delicious, coral coloured sauce that's mildly spiced and slightly tangy, a perfect partner to the salty sweetness of shellfish. Sun-blush tomatoes, which are roasted and usually sold in oil, have a sweeter flavour and softer texture than sun-dried tomatoes. If you cannot find them, substitute 2 tablespoons of sun-dried tomato paste.

PREPARATION TIME: 12 minutes

SERVES: 8

100 g (3½ oz) sun-blush tomatoes, drained

1 quantity Mayonnaise (see page 22)

4 tablespoons soured cream

1 tablespoon brandy

1 teaspoon Tabasco sauce

salt

1 Put the sun-blush tomatoes into a food processor or blender and chop into small pieces, scraping down the mixture from the sides of the bowl if necessary.

2 Add the mayonnaise, soured cream, brandy, Tabasco and a little salt and blend until evenly combined. Alternatively, finely chop the tomatoes by hand and mix them in a bowl with the remaining ingredients.

3 Add a little more salt, if you like, then turn the sauce into a small serving dish. Cover and chill until ready to serve.

Variations: Use a splash of Pernod or Pastis instead of the brandy, or leave out the alcohol altogether. To make a Thousand Island Dressing, add 1 finely chopped hard-boiled egg, 12 finely chopped green olives and 2 tablespoons chopped chives.

Hollandaise sauce

Hollandaise is a thick, velvety sauce. It perfects a springtime starter, generously spooned over fresh asparagus spears or new potatoes, broccoli, pan-fried fish or egg dishes. It requires just a little patience and needs to be made within about half an hour of serving.

PREPARATION TIME: 10 minutes

COOKING TIME: 10 minutes

SERVES: 6

2 tablespoons white wine vinegar

1 bay leaf

½ teaspoon black peppercorns

1 tablespoon water

3 egg yolks

200 g (7 oz) unsalted butter, softened and cut into 1 cm (½ inch) cubes

salt and pepper

1 Put the vinegar, bay leaf, peppercorns and water in a small, heavy-based saucepan. Heat until bubbling and simmer until the liquid has reduced by half.

2 Heat a medium-sized pan containing about 5 cm (2 inches) of water until simmering. Put the egg yolks in a heatproof bowl that sits comfortably over the pan without the base touching the water. Strain the vinegar mixture into the yolks and whisk lightly to combine.

3 Whisk in a cube of butter. As soon as it has melted into the sauce, add another cube and whisk again until absorbed. Continue adding the remaining butter, one cube at a time, until the sauce is thick and glossy. Season with a little salt and check the flavour.

Cook's tip: Hollandaise will keep for up to about 30 minutes. Turn off the heat but leave the bowl over the pan and cover it with a lid. Lightly whisk before serving, adding a dash of water if it has over-thickened and reheat gently if necessary.

Variation:

Hollandaise with red pepper and thyme
In this recipe, a smooth red pepper paste adds sweetness, tang and plenty of colour to a buttery Hollandaise sauce. This sauce is particularly good with poached fish, or spooned over almost any freshly cooked shellfish to make a fabulous starter or light lunch.

PREPARATION TIME: 15 minutes

COOKING TIME: 15 minutes

SERVES: 6

250 g (8 oz) unsalted butter, softened

1 large red pepper, deseeded and finely chopped

several sprigs of fresh thyme

1 tablespoon red or white wine vinegar

3 egg yolks

salt and pepper

1 Melt 25 g (1 oz) of the butter in a frying pan. Cut the remainder into 1 cm (½ inch) cubes. Add the red pepper to the frying pan with the thyme sprigs. Cook very gently for about 5 minutes until the pepper is very soft and tender. Tip the mixture into a sieve set over a bowl and push as much of the pepper through the sieve as you can using the back of a metal spoon.

2 Put the vinegar and egg yolks into a bowl and make the sauce following steps 2 and 3 (see opposite). Whisk in the pepper paste once all the butter has been added. Season with salt and pepper to taste and serve.

Hollandaise sauce with capers and herbs

Finely chopped capers, parsley and chives give this sauce a fresh tangy flavour, rather like a hot Tartare sauce. Other freshly chopped herbs such as basil, chervil, fennel and dill make equally successful alternatives, great for serving with fish.

PREPARATION TIME: 10 minutes

COOKING TIME: 10 minutes

SERVES: 6

2 tablespoons capers

2 tablespoons finely chopped flat leaf parsley

2 tablespoons finely chopped chives

1–2 tablespoons lemon juice

3 egg yolks

200 g (7 oz) unsalted butter, cut into 1 cm (½ inch) cubes

salt and pepper

1 Rinse and drain the capers and pat dry on kitchen paper. Chop them finely and mix with the herbs.

2 Put 1 tablespoon of the lemon juice into a bowl with the egg yolks and make the sauce following steps 2 and 3 of the Hollandaise recipe on page 26. Add the chopped capers and herbs with the last of the butter. Season with salt and pepper to taste, adding a little more lemon juice for extra tang, if you like.

Béarnaise sauce

Béarnaise sauce is simply a Hollandaise sauce aromatically flavoured with shallots and herbs. It can also be served with vegetables but is at its best poured over pan-fried beef, salmon or cod steaks.

PREPARATION TIME: 15 minutes

COOKING TIME: 10 minutes

SERVES: 6

15 g (½ oz) fresh tarragon sprigs

2 shallots, finely chopped

3 tablespoons tarragon or white wine vinegar

½ teaspoon black peppercorns

1 tablespoon water

3 egg yolks

200 g (7 oz) unsalted butter, softened and cut into 1 cm (½ inch) cubes

salt and pepper

1 Pull the tarragon leaves from the stalks and roughly chop. Put a quarter of the chopped tarragon into a small saucepan with the shallots, vinegar, peppercorns and water. Bring to a bubble and cook until the liquid has reduced to about 1 tablespoon.

2 Follow steps 2 and 3 of the Hollandaise Sauce recipe on page 26, adding the remaining chopped tarragon with the last of the butter. Season with salt and pepper to taste and serve.

Beurre blanc
Beurre blanc is an emulsion sauce like Hollandaise, but it is made without eggs. Delicate and buttery, it makes a lovely smooth sauce for spooning over fish and shellfish. For a beurre rouge sauce, substitute red wine and red wine vinegar for the white.

PREPARATION TIME: 5 minutes

COOKING TIME: 5 minutes

SERVES: 4

2 small shallots, finely chopped

3 tablespoons white wine vinegar

3 tablespoons dry white wine

2 tablespoons double cream

125 g (4 oz) unsalted butter, chilled and cut into 1 cm (½ inch) cubes

salt and pepper

1 Put the shallots, vinegar and wine in a small heavy-based saucepan and cook until the liquid has reduced to about 2 tablespoons. Add the cream and let it bubble until slightly reduced.

2 Reduce the heat to its lowest setting and gradually whisk in the butter, a cube at a time, until the sauce is smooth and velvety. (If you feel that the mixture is getting too hot, remove the pan from the heat while you add a little more butter.) Season with salt and pepper and serve immediately.

Variation: For a Herb Beurre Blanc, whisk in 2 tablespoons finely chopped herbs such as tarragon, chervil or dill.

Espagnole sauce

Dark, rich and packed with flavour, a traditional Espagnole sauce, the classic accompaniment to red meats and game, is the result of long simmered stocks and a laborious sauce-making technique. This is a simplified version that relies on a good beef stock and slow, gentle cooking.

PREPARATION TIME: 15 minutes

COOKING TIME: 1 hour

SERVES: 4–5

25 g (1 oz) butter

2 rashers of rindless streaky bacon, chopped

2 shallots, chopped

1 carrot, chopped

1 celery stick, chopped

50 g (2 oz) mushrooms, chopped

2 tablespoons plain flour

600 ml (1 pint) Beef Stock (see page 10)

1 bouquet garni

2 tablespoons tomato paste

1 tablespoon sherry

salt and pepper

1 Melt the butter in a heavy-based saucepan until bubbling. Add the bacon and fry gently until beginning to colour. Add the vegetables and cook until well browned.

2 Add the flour and cook, stirring with a wooden spoon, for 3 minutes until the roux is dark brown. Remove from the heat and slowly stir in the beef stock.

3 Return the pan to the heat and add the bouquet garni, tomato paste and a little salt and pepper. Bring just to the boil, reduce the heat, then partially cover the pan with a lid and cook very gently for about 45 minutes, skimming if necessary.

4 Strain the sauce through a sieve into a clean pan, pressing the mixture to extract the juices. Add the sherry and heat gently. Add water if the sauce is too thick (it should thinly coat the back of a wooden spoon). Check the seasoning and serve hot, or cool and chill for up to 4 days.

Ginger and orange sauce *This is a lighter version of the traditional Espagnole sauce. It is lightly sweetened with orange and flavoured with shreds of fresh root ginger, and adds a piquant touch to lamb steaks, chicken or duck breasts.*

PREPARATION TIME: 10 minutes

COOKING TIME: 35 minutes

SERVES: 4–5

25 g (1 oz) piece fresh root ginger, peeled

½ bunch spring onions

25 g (1 oz) butter

1 celery stick, chopped

2 tablespoons plain flour

450 ml (¾ pint) Chicken or Vegetable Stock
(see page 12)

finely grated rind and juice of 1 orange

several sprigs of thyme

1 tablespoon sherry

salt and pepper

1 Finely shred the ginger. Trim the spring onions and finely chop, keeping the green and white parts separate.

2 Melt the butter in a large heavy-based saucepan until bubbling. Add the celery and the white parts of the onions and fry gently for 3 minutes. Add the flour and cook, stirring, for 2 minutes until pale golden.

3 Remove from the heat and gradually blend in the stock. Return to the heat and add the orange rind and juice and thyme sprigs. Bring to the boil, then reduce the heat and simmer very gently, partially covered with a lid, for 30 minutes.

4 Complete the sauce, following step 4 (see opposite), stirring in the ginger and chopped green spring onions when reheating.

Anchovy and pickled walnut sauce

Salty anchovies and tangy pickled walnuts make a good partnership in stuffings and pâtés, and are equally good in a sauce to serve with steak. Pickled walnuts are usually available in jars in food stores, alongside the pickles and chutneys.

PREPARATION TIME: 3 minutes

COOKING TIME: 5 minutes

SERVES: 4–5

3 pickled walnuts, drained

6 anchovy fillets

1 quantity Espagnole Sauce (see page 30)

3 tablespoons chopped parsley

salt and pepper

1 Finely chop the pickled walnuts and anchovy fillets.

2 Put the sauce, walnuts and anchovies in a saucepan and heat through gently for 5 minutes, stirring frequently.

3 Sprinkle in the parsley and check the seasoning. Serve hot.

Bacon and baby onion sauce *This richly*

flavoured sauce is delicious lavished over portions of freshly cooked chicken, or as a 'cook in' sauce for chicken portions. It's also good with sausages or homemade herby meatballs.

PREPARATION TIME: 15 minutes

COOKING TIME: 40 minutes

SERVES: 6

150 g (5 oz) smoked back bacon

25 g (1 oz) butter

1 tablespoon vegetable oil

100 g (3½ oz) chestnut mushrooms, chopped

250 g (8 oz) baby onions, peeled and left whole

1 quantity Espagnole Sauce (see page 30)

salt and pepper

2 tablespoons roughly chopped flat leaf parsley, to garnish

1 Cut the bacon into small pieces. Melt the butter with the oil in a large heavy-based frying pan until bubbling. Add the mushrooms and fry quickly for 3–4 minutes until lightly browned then remove them with a slotted spoon. Add the bacon and onions to the pan and fry gently for 5 minutes, stirring with a wooden spoon until browned.

2 Add the Espagnole sauce and bring just to the boil. Reduce the heat and simmer gently for 25 minutes until the onions are tender.

3 Add the mushrooms and cook for a further 5 minutes. Season with salt and pepper to taste and serve sprinkled with the parsley.

Chasseur sauce

This is another delicious variation on Espagnole Sauce, but lighter and quicker to make. If you're making it to accompany beef, stick to the rich beef stock, but if it's for chicken or poultry, use a lighter chicken stock.

PREPARATION TIME: 10 minutes

COOKING TIME: 25 minutes

SERVES: 4

40 g (1½ oz) butter

200 g (7 oz) button mushrooms, thinly sliced

2 shallots, finely chopped

2 teaspoons plain flour

150 ml (¼ pint) dry white wine

300 ml (½ pint) Beef or Chicken Stock (see pages 10 and 12)

2 tablespoons finely chopped chervil or tarragon

1 tablespoon brandy (optional)

salt and pepper

1 Melt the butter in a large heavy-based saucepan until bubbling. Add the mushrooms and shallots and fry quickly for 5 minutes until lightly browned. Remove the mushrooms with a slotted spoon, leaving any small pieces of shallot in the pan.

2 Add the flour and cook, stirring constantly, for 2 minutes until it begins to darken in colour. Remove from the heat and gradually blend in the wine, then the stock.

3 Return to the heat, bring to the boil, then simmer gently for 15 minutes until the sauce is slightly thickened. Stir in the mushrooms, chervil or tarragon, brandy, if using, and salt and pepper to taste. Serve hot.

Fresh herb butter

Rich and delicious, flavoured butters make some of the best and simplest sauces as they melt irresistibly over grilled, baked or pan-fried meat or fish. They're easy to make, can be prepared ahead, and even frozen. Melt them over hot vegetables, swirl into bean or lentil soups or lavish on hot buttered toast.

PREPARATION TIME: 3 minutes, plus chilling
SERVES: 4–6

100 g (3½ oz) unsalted butter, softened
¼ teaspoon salt
2 tablespoons finely chopped parsley
2 tablespoons finely snipped chives
2 teaspoons lemon juice
pepper

1 Put the butter into a small bowl with the salt, parsley, chives, lemon juice and several grinds of black pepper. (Unsalted butter is best, but if you only have salted, leave out the additional salt.)

2 Beat the mixture with a wooden spoon until evenly combined.

3 If you're not using the butter immediately it can be shaped into a roll and chilled for up to 2 days, or frozen for several weeks, a worthwhile way of using up a large quantity of fresh herbs. Simply turn the mixture onto a strip of greaseproof paper and bring the sides of the paper up over the butter, gently squeezing it into a sausage shape about 3 cm (1¼ inches) in diameter.

4 Chill or freeze the butter until you are ready to use it. If it is frozen, leave it at room temperature for 20–30 minutes before serving.

Variation:

Red pepper, serrano and paprika butter *Colourful and warmly spiced, this butter has a Spanish flavour that's well suited to chicken, pork and rabbit dishes. Use a pointed red pepper if possible as it has a stronger, less watery flavour than ordinary ones.*

PREPARATION TIME: 5 minutes

SERVES: 5–6

½ small pointed red pepper, deseeded

50 g (2 oz) Serrano ham, finely chopped

1 teaspoon ground paprika, preferably smoked

100 g (3½ oz) unsalted butter, softened

¼ teaspoon sea salt

1 Chop the red pepper as finely as possible and put it into a bowl with the ham, paprika, butter and salt.

2 Complete the butter following steps 2 and 3 of Fresh Herb Butter (see opposite) and chill for at least 30 minutes before serving to let the flavours mingle.

Horseradish butter
Fresh horseradish is not widely available, but a jar of hot, grated horseradish makes a good substitute. Horseradish butter is particularly good with white and oily fish, steak and vegetables. Its flavour often intensifies during storage so add with caution to any dish.

PREPARATION TIME: 5 minutes

SERVES: 4–6

100 g (3½ oz) unsalted butter, softened

¼ teaspoon sea salt

1 tablespoon finely grated fresh horseradish

2 tablespoons crème fraîche

1 Put the butter, salt and horseradish into a small bowl and beat with a wooden spoon until evenly combined. Stir in the crème fraîche.

2 If you are not using it immediately, follow steps 3 and 4 of Fresh Herb Butter on page 34 for either chilling or freezing.

Prawn butter
Sweet, meaty prawns, whizzed in a food processor or blender, give this rich, creamy butter a very smooth, almost mousse-like texture. Serve it with white fish and chicken dishes or, for a real treat, spread on thick slices of hot toast.

PREPARATION TIME: 5 minutes

SERVES: 6

250 g (8 oz) peeled prawns, thawed and thoroughly drained if frozen

¼ teaspoon cayenne pepper

100 g (3½ oz) unsalted butter, softened

1 teaspoon sun-dried tomato paste

1 Put the prawns in a food processor or blender with the cayenne pepper and blend to a paste. Add the butter and tomato paste and blend until smooth, scraping down the mixture from the sides of the bowl if necessary.

2 If you are not using it immediately, follow steps 3 and 4 of Fresh Herb Butter on page 34 for either chilling or freezing.

Chilli spice butter

This is one of the most versatile butters of all, perfect for perking up plain fish and poultry or topping barbecued meat, green and root vegetables, or new potatoes. It's also a useful freezer standby for stirring into pasta dishes, soups and vegetable stews, or even a simple risotto.

PREPARATION TIME: 10 minutes, plus chilling

SERVES: 4–6

2 teaspoons cumin seeds

1 teaspoon coriander seeds

1 red chilli, deseeded and finely chopped

2 red or white spring onions, trimmed and finely chopped

1 plump garlic clove, crushed

100 g (3½ oz) unsalted butter, softened

¼ teaspoon sea salt

2 tablespoons finely chopped parsley or coriander

1 Put the cumin and coriander seeds into a small frying pan and heat gently for about 1 minute until just beginning to colour. Transfer to a mortar and grind until lightly crushed.

2 Tip into a bowl and add the chilli, onions, garlic, butter, salt and parsley or coriander.

3 Complete the butter, following steps 2 and 3 of Fresh Herb Butter on page 34 and chill for at least 30 minutes before serving to let the flavours mingle.

These sauces are not specifically for vegetarians, but for eating with vegetable dishes, recognizing the fact that vegetables now play a more prominent role in our everyday meals. A plate of healthy steamed vegetables can be lifted enormously if it is bathed in an aromatic Gribiche Sauce. Or, for a fabulous starter or light lunch dish, try a selection of raw spring vegetables, served with Salsa Verde, which is packed with distinctive flavours such as garlic, capers and anchovies. The sauces in this chapter focus on aromatic ingredients and have plenty of colour and texture to complement the vegetables they partner, but you needn't make them exclusively for vegetables – many of them would be equally at home with cheese, egg, meat and fish dishes.

Gribiche sauce

Like Mayonnaise, Gribiche is made by gradually working oil into eggs. In this case, cooked egg yolks are used so the sauce has quite a strong flavour. It is delicious with hot or cold vegetables, particularly asparagus. The egg yolk paste can be made in advance but the sauce is best completed just before serving.

PREPARATION TIME: 15 minutes

SERVES: 4

4 hard-boiled egg yolks

1 teaspoon Dijon mustard

200 ml (7 fl oz) light olive oil

1–2 tablespoons white wine vinegar

2 tablespoons capers, rinsed and roughly chopped

2 tablespoons chives, snipped

white of 1 egg, chopped (optional)

salt and pepper

extra snipped chives or chive flowers, to garnish

1 Pound the egg yolks, mustard and a little salt and pepper using a large pestle and mortar. Alternatively, put the ingredients into a food processor or blender and mix together lightly.

2 Drizzle in a little of the oil, mixing well until blended. Keep drizzling in more oil until you have incorporated about half and the mixture makes a thick paste. Add 1 tablespoon of the vinegar.

3 Gradually blend in the remaining oil. (Don't add the oil too quickly or the sauce might separate.)

4 Turn the sauce into a bowl or jug and stir in the capers and chives, then add a little more vinegar and salt and pepper if necessary.

5 Spoon the sauce over vegetables and sprinkle with the egg white, if using, and chives or chive flowers to garnish.

Gribiche sauce

Great with: *steamed or roasted asparagus, broccoli, cauliflower, courgettes and beans. Also with ham, salmon or trout*

Salsa verde
This intensely flavoured sauce is packed with aromatic ingredients such as fresh herbs, olives, capers and anchovies. Served cold, it's a summery sauce you can make in advance or a dip for cooked or raw vegetables. Wrap well and chill for up to 8 hours.

PREPARATION TIME: 5 minutes, plus chilling

SERVES: 6

25 g (1 oz) flat leaf parsley

15 g (½ oz) mixed basil, chives and mint

2 garlic cloves, roughly chopped

15 g (½ oz) pitted green olives

1 tablespoon capers, rinsed

2 teaspoons wholegrain mustard

3 anchovy fillets

3–4 teaspoons lemon juice

125 ml (4 fl oz) extra virgin olive oil

salt and pepper

1 Tear the herbs into smaller sprigs without discarding the stalks. Put them into a food processor or blender with the garlic, olives, capers, mustard and anchovy fillets. Add 3 teaspoons of the lemon juice.

2 Blend the ingredients together until finely chopped. Gradually blend in the oil to form a chunky sauce. Season with salt and pepper, adding a little extra lemon juice to sharpen the flavour if you like. Turn into a small serving bowl and chill until ready to serve.

Chickpea and chilli sauce
The yogurt and spices in this unconventional sauce give it a slightly North African flavour which makes it particularly suitable for serving with outdoor summery dishes, vegetarian or otherwise. It's blended to a smooth, thick consistency but you can leave it chunkier if you want a sauce with more texture.

PREPARATION TIME: 10 minutes

COOKING TIME: 2 minutes

SERVES: 6

3 tablespoons sunflower oil

2 tablespoons walnut oil

2 teaspoons cumin seeds, lightly crushed

½ teaspoon crushed dried chillies

400 g (13 oz) can chickpeas, rinsed and drained

2 tablespoons tahini

1 plump garlic clove, roughly chopped

2 spring onions, roughly chopped

150 ml (¼ pint) natural yogurt

3–4 tablespoons milk

salt

1 Heat the oils in a small frying pan with the cumin seeds and chillies and cook very gently for 2 minutes. Remove from the heat.

2 Put the chickpeas, tahini, garlic and spring onions into a food processor or blender and tip in the oil and spices. Blend to a chunky paste, scraping the mixture down from the sides of the bowl if necessary.

3 Add the yogurt, milk and a little salt and blend to a smooth consistency, adding a little more milk if the sauce is still very thick. Serve cold or warm through very gently in a small pan. Don't overheat the sauce or the yogurt will separate.

Fennel and mascarpone sauce *Buttery sautéed fennel and melting mascarpone make a fabulous combination that's great for topping a simple vegetable gratin or to serve with egg dishes. Take care not to overheat the mascarpone as it might lose its smooth consistency.*

PREPARATION TIME: 10 minutes

COOKING TIME: 10 minutes

SERVES: 4

1 small fennel bulb

25 g (1 oz) butter

1 small onion, finely chopped

1 tablespoon lemon juice

150 ml (¼ pint) Vegetable Stock (see page 12)

200 g (7 oz) mascarpone cheese

salt and pepper

1 Trim the fennel, chopping and reserving any feathery fronds. Finely chop the fennel bulb. Melt the butter in a heavy-based saucepan until bubbling. Fry the fennel and onion very gently, stirring frequently, for 6–8 minutes until they are very tender.

2 Add the lemon juice, stock, mascarpone and a little salt and pepper and cook very gently until the mascarpone has melted and the sauce is hot. Check the seasoning and stir in any chopped fennel fronds. Serve hot.

Hot harissa sauce

A quick and easy sauce with plenty of flavour. Use the entire mixture to stir into sautéed vegetables and beans or as a wonderful couscous topping, or zip up soups and stews with smaller quantities. It can be kept in the refrigerator, tightly wrapped, for up to 5 days.

PREPARATION TIME: 10 minutes, plus chilling

COOKING TIME: 5 minutes

SERVES: 4–6

1 tablespoon coriander seeds

1 teaspoon caraway seeds

3 tablespoons light olive oil

1 red pepper, deseeded and roughly chopped

1 small red onion, roughly chopped

1 red chilli, deseeded and chopped

3 garlic cloves, chopped

4 tablespoons coriander leaves, torn into pieces

½ teaspoon celery salt

150 ml (5 oz) passata

1 Using a pestle and mortar, grind the coriander and caraway seeds until lightly crushed. Alternatively, use a small bowl and the end of a rolling pin.

2 Tip the seeds into a small frying pan and add the olive oil, red pepper and onion. Cook very gently for 5 minutes until the vegetables are soft.

3 Transfer the mixture to a food processor or blender and add the chilli, garlic, coriander, celery salt and passata.

4 Blend until smooth, scraping the mixture down from the sides of the bowl if necessary. Transfer to a serving bowl and cover with clingfilm. Chill until ready to serve.

Hot harissa sauce

Great with: *couscous and mixed vegetable stews. Also for topping grilled tomatoes, lamb, chicken or fish*

Hot and sour chilli sauce
Tamarind is the fruit of the Asian tamarind tree and is readily available in jars as a thick paste. It has a slightly sour, fruity flavour and usually needs sweetening in sauces to reduce its sharpness.

PREPARATION TIME: 10 minutes

COOKING TIME: 15 minutes

SERVES: 4

1 lemongrass stalk

1 tablespoon sunflower oil

3 shallots, finely chopped

3 cm (1¼ inch) piece fresh root ginger, peeled and finely chopped

150 ml (¼ pint) Vegetable Stock (see page 12)

¼ teaspoon crushed dried chillies

2 tablespoons tamarind paste

juice of ½ lime

2 tablespoons dark muscovado sugar

salt

1 Trim the ends from the lemongrass, then chop the stalk as finely as possible. Heat the oil in a frying pan or wok and gently fry the shallots, ginger and lemongrass for 3 minutes until softened but not browned.

2 Add the stock, then stir in the dried chillies, tamarind paste, lime juice, sugar and a little salt.

3 Bring the sauce to the boil and let it bubble over a moderate heat for about 10 minutes until slightly reduced. Serve hot.

Spicy gazpacho sauce
The vibrant, invigorating flavour of Gazpacho, the classic Spanish soup, converts easily into a deliciously refreshing summer sauce that can be whizzed up in a matter of minutes. It's a light and easy palate-cleanser.

PREPARATION TIME: 10 minutes

COOKING TIME: 5 minutes

SERVES: 6

500 g (1 lb) ripe tomatoes

¼ cucumber, peeled and roughly sliced

1 small red pepper, deseeded and roughly chopped

2 celery sticks, roughly chopped

small handful of coriander leaves

2 teaspoons lemon juice

1 tablespoon sun-dried tomato paste

1 teaspoon chilli oil

salt

1 Skin the tomatoes (see page 9) and roughly chop them.

2 Put the tomatoes into a saucepan over a low heat and bring to the boil, breaking up the pieces with a wooden spoon. Cook gently for about 5 minutes until the mixture is thick and pulpy and most of the juice has evaporated.

3 Tip the tomatoes into a food processor or blender and add all the remaining ingredients. Blend until smooth, scraping the mixture down from the sides of the bowl if necessary. Check the seasoning and leave to cool or return the soup to the saucepan and reheat gently if serving warm.

Spicy fruit and nut sauce *This blended*
sauce combines aromatic seeds with nuts and dried fruit to make a rich,
sweet and spicy sauce with a slightly North African flavour, perfect with
chargrilled vegetables and couscous. It can be made in advance and
chilled overnight.

PREPARATION TIME: 10 minutes

COOKING TIME: 2 minutes

SERVES: 4–5

2 teaspoons cardamom pods

2 teaspoons coriander seeds

½ teaspoon dried chilli flakes

15 g (½ oz) chopped almonds

15 g (½ oz) shelled pistachio nuts

75 g (3 oz) ready-to-eat prunes

50 g (2 oz) ready-to-eat dried apricots

250 ml (8 fl oz) **Vegetable Stock** (see page 12)

salt

1 Crush the cardamom pods using a pestle and mortar, then pick out and discard the shells. Add the coriander seeds and chilli flakes and crush fairly finely.

2 Transfer the spices to a food processor or blender and add the nuts and dried fruit. Blend to a thick paste, scraping down the mixture from the sides of the bowl if necessary.

3 Add the stock and a little salt and blend again until fairly smooth. Tip the mixture into a small saucepan and heat through gently for 2–3 minutes. Serve warm.

Pasta sauces are just about the easiest of all, their popularity and simplicity brought about by our need to provide meals that can be assembled in minutes. The range of pasta sauces is so extensive that it's impossible to include them all here, but the choice extends from the quickest of all, recipes such as Goats' Cheese and Pine Nut Sauce, to the best fresh tomato sauce and a really authentic-tasting Bolognese. Pasta sauces are good at any time of year; they can be light and healthy or rich and totally indulgent, however the mood takes you.

Sauces for pasta

Puttanesca sauce

This intense Italian tomato sauce has plenty of extra flavours such as black olives, anchovies and chillies. Thick and richly flavoured, it's great tossed with almost any pasta, especially spaghetti, for a deliciously quick supper dish. Scatter with Parmesan cheese if you like.

PREPARATION TIME: 15 minutes

COOKING TIME: 15 minutes

SERVES: 4

4 tablespoons olive oil

1 onion, finely chopped

3 garlic cloves, crushed

1 small red chilli, deseeded and finely chopped

6 anchovy fillets, chopped

2 x 400 g (13 oz) cans chopped tomatoes

½ teaspoon caster sugar

75 g (3 oz) black olives, pitted and finely chopped

small handful of basil leaves

2 tablespoons capers, rinsed and drained

salt

freshly grated Parmesan cheese, to serve (optional)

1 Heat the oil in a heavy-based saucepan. Add the onion and fry gently for 3–4 minutes until softened. Add the garlic and chilli and cook for a further minute.

2 Add the anchovy fillets, tomatoes, sugar and black olives, and bring to the boil. Reduce the heat and simmer gently for 10 minutes until the sauce is thick.

3 Add the basil leaves, capers and a little salt and stir through for 1 minute. Serve hot, sprinkled with Parmesan cheese, if you like.

Puttanesca sauce

Great with: *any type of pasta, chicken or fish, or poured over roasted vegetables*

Roasted pepper sauce

Unlike most sauces, this one's baked in the oven until it's sweet and caramelized before it's lightly blended to a fine consistency. It's delicious served as it is with spaghetti or linguini, or with some chopped mozzarella stirred in just before serving.

PREPARATION TIME: 10 minutes

COOKING TIME: 50 minutes

SERVES: 4

3 large red peppers, deseeded and roughly chopped

1 yellow or orange pepper, deseeded and roughly chopped

1 red onion, chopped

2 garlic cloves, sliced

3 tomatoes, skinned (see page 9) and quartered

4 large oregano sprigs, roughly chopped

5 tablespoons extra virgin olive oil

5 tablespoons white wine or water

salt and pepper

1 Put the peppers, onion, garlic, tomatoes and oregano into a large roasting tin.

Drizzle with 3 tablespoons of the olive oil and a little salt and pepper and toss the ingredients together well. Roast in a preheated oven, 220°C (425°F), Gas Mark 7, for about 50 minutes until the vegetables are thoroughly browned around the edges. Turn the ingredients once or twice during roasting.

2 Tip the mixture into a food processor or blender. Stir the wine or water into the roasting tin to scrape up the pan juices and add to the pepper mixture. Blend very lightly so the vegetables become chopped and pulpy.

3 Return the sauce to the tin with the remaining oil and reheat for 2 minutes. Check the seasoning and serve hot.

Tomato and pancetta sauce

A fresh tomato sauce is only worth making if you can get hold of really tasty, well-flavoured tomatoes. Even better is a glut of home-grown ones so you can make large quantities for the freezer.

PREPARATION TIME: 15 minutes

COOKING TIME: 25 minutes

SERVES: 4–6

1 kg (2 lb) ripe tomatoes

75 ml (3 fl oz) extra virgin olive oil

1 large onion, finely chopped

1 garlic clove, finely chopped

2 tablespoons chopped oregano

75 g (3 oz) pancetta, chopped

salt and pepper

1 Skin the tomatoes (see page 9) and roughly chop them.

2 Heat the oil in a large heavy-based saucepan and add the onion and garlic. Fry over a gentle heat, stirring frequently, until the onion is soft. Add the tomatoes, oregano and a little salt and pepper.

3 Bring to a bubble, then reduce the heat and let the sauce cook gently, covered with a lid, for about 15 minutes until thickened and pulpy. Break up the tomatoes frequently during cooking.

4 Meanwhile dry-fry the pancetta in a small pan until crisp. Add to the cooked sauce and check the seasoning.

Pesto

Making pesto traditionally with a pestle and mortar fills the air with the wonderful fragrance of crushed basil leaves, but is more time consuming than the quick and easy food processor method used here. Freshly made pesto has numerous uses, most commonly as a pasta sauce but also to flavour soups, stews and risottos.

PREPARATION TIME: 5 minutes

SERVES: 4

50 g (2 oz) fresh basil, including stalks

50 g (2 oz) pine nuts

65 g (2½ oz) freshly grated Parmesan cheese

2 garlic cloves, chopped

125 ml (4 fl oz) olive oil

salt and pepper

1 Tear the basil into pieces and put it into a food processor with the pine nuts, Parmesan and garlic.

2 Blend lightly until the nuts and cheese are broken into small pieces, scraping the mixture down from the sides of the bowl if necessary.

3 Add the olive oil and a little salt and blend to a thick paste. Stir into freshly cooked pasta or turn into a bowl and refrigerate. It can be kept, covered, for up to 5 days.

Variation: To make Red Pesto, drain 125g (4 oz) sun-dried tomatoes in oil, chop them into small pieces and add to the food processor instead of the basil.

Bolognese sauce

Combining Italian-style spicy sausages with the more familiar minced beef gives this sauce a rich meaty flavour reminiscent of the traditional sauce served in Bologna. Allow time for long, gentle cooking to tenderize the meat and let the flavours mingle.

PREPARATION TIME: 15 minutes

COOKING TIME: 1¼ hours

SERVES: 4–5

25 g (1 oz) butter

2 tablespoons olive oil

1 onion, finely chopped

2 celery sticks, finely chopped

2 garlic cloves, crushed

500 g (1 lb) lean minced beef

200 g (7 oz) spicy Italian sausages, skinned

300 ml (½ pint) red or white wine

400 g (13 oz) can chopped tomatoes

1 teaspoon caster sugar

2 bay leaves

1 teaspoon dried oregano

2 tablespoons sun-dried tomato paste

salt and pepper

1 Melt the butter with the oil in a large heavy-based saucepan and gently fry the onion and celery for 5 minutes. Add the garlic, beef and skinned sausages, and cook until they are lightly coloured, breaking up the beef and the sausages with a wooden spoon.

2 Add the wine and let it bubble for 1–2 minutes until slightly evaporated. Add the tomatoes, sugar, bay leaves, oregano, tomato paste and a little salt and pepper and bring just to the boil. Reduce the heat to its lowest setting, cover the pan with a lid and cook for about 1 hour, stirring occasionally, until thick and pulpy.

Bolognese sauce

Great with: *tagliatelle, linguini or spaghetti, sprinkled with grated Parmesan cheese. Also for lasagne and cannelloni*

Goats' cheese and pine nut sauce

For a quick and easy, meat-free supper with plenty of texture and flavour, this sauce is difficult to beat and needs nothing more than a leafy herb salad to accompany it. Try it with fresh egg or spinach pasta or as a sauce for meat- or cheese-stuffed tortellini.

PREPARATION TIME: 10 minutes

COOKING TIME: 5 minutes

SERVES: 4

1 leek

25 g (1 oz) butter

75 g (3 oz) pine nuts

2 garlic cloves, thinly sliced

300 ml (½ pint) single cream

finely grated rind and juice of 1 lemon

150 g (5 oz) firm goats' cheese, crumbled

salt and pepper

1 Wash and trim the leek, then shred it as finely as possible. Melt the butter in a frying pan and gently fry the pine nuts until they are beginning to colour, about 2 minutes. Add the garlic and shredded leek and fry for 1 more minute.

2 Add the cream, lemon rind and juice to the pan and crumble in the goats' cheese. Season with a little salt and pepper and stir for 1–2 minutes until the cream is bubbling and the cheese has started to melt. Toss with lightly drained, hot pasta and serve immediately.

Olive and caper tapenade

This richly flavoured sauce is really more of a paste that's transformed into a delicious sauce when blended into freshly cooked pasta. It is a great recipe to make ahead and store in the refrigerator for a quick and easy supper dish. Any leftovers make a good topping for crostini.

PREPARATION TIME: 5 minutes

SERVES: 4

100 g (3½ oz) pitted black olives

4 tablespoons capers, rinsed and drained

50 g (2 oz) sun-dried tomatoes in oil, drained

6 anchovy fillets, drained

1 teaspoon fennel seeds, lightly crushed

small handful of flat leaf parsley, roughly chopped

small handful of basil, roughly chopped

150 ml (¼ pint) olive oil

salt and pepper

freshly grated Parmesan cheese, to serve (optional)

1 Put the olives, capers, tomatoes, anchovy fillets and fennel seeds into a food processor or blender and blend to a paste, scraping down the mixture from the sides of the bowl if necessary.

2 Add the parsley, basil, oil and a little salt and pepper and blend very briefly until the herbs are finely chopped and all the ingredients are blended.

3 Stir the sauce into lightly drained pasta and serve sprinkled with Parmesan, if you like.

Walnut, dolcelatte and crème fraîche sauce

Walnuts make a great pasta sauce as they provide plenty of texture and flavour, without the need for many other ingredients. This simple sauce is very rich, so serve it in small portions with penne or pasta twists and a tomato or leafy salad accompaniment.

PREPARATION TIME: 10 minutes

COOKING TIME: 5 minutes

SERVES: 3–4

2 tablespoons walnut oil

2 garlic cloves, crushed

100 g (3½ oz) walnut pieces, chopped

150 g (5 oz) dolcelatte cheese

200 ml (7 fl oz) crème fraîche

2 tablespoons chopped flat leaf parsley

salt and pepper

1 Heat the oil in a frying pan and gently fry the garlic for 1 minute. Add the walnuts and fry for a further minute.

2 Crumble or break the cheese into the garlic and walnuts, then spoon in the crème fraîche and parsley. Add a little salt and pepper and heat for 1–2 minutes until the cheese is melting but still retains some texture. Toss the sauce with hot pasta or spoon over pasta on serving plates.

Smoked salmon and dill sauce

This sauce provides a perfect use for packs of smoked salmon trimmings, which are very cheap but taste just as good as the more expensive choice pieces. Conveniently, the trimmings are also the right size for stirring into a delicious pasta sauce.

PREPARATION TIME: 10 minutes

COOKING TIME: 15 minutes

SERVES: 4

25 g (1 oz) butter

1 fennel bulb, finely chopped

2 small courgettes, diced

2 garlic cloves, crushed

100 ml (3½ fl oz) white wine

100 g (3½ oz) fresh or frozen peas

small handful dill, chopped

250 g (8 oz) mascarpone cheese

150 g (5 oz) smoked salmon, cut into pieces

salt and pepper

1 Melt the butter in a large saucepan and fry the fennel and courgettes very gently for 6–8 minutes until soft but not browned. Add the garlic and fry for 2 minutes.

2 Add the wine and a little salt and pepper and bring to the boil. Let the sauce bubble for a minute until the wine is slightly reduced.

3 Transfer the sauce to a food processor or blender and blend very lightly until it is pulpy but not smooth.

4 Tip the sauce back into the pan and add the peas, dill, mascarpone and salmon. Cook gently until heated through. Check the seasoning and serve hot.

Smoked salmon and dill sauce

Great with: *tagliatelle or spaghetti*

Chicken liver, mushroom and marsala sauce
Marsala and fruit vinegar give a sweet tang to this sauce, balancing the richness of the chicken livers. Serve it with fresh spinach or mushroom tagliatelle for a light lunch or supper.

PREPARATION TIME: 10 minutes

COOKING TIME: 10 minutes

SERVES: 2

250 g (8 oz) chicken livers

25 g (1oz) butter

1 tablespoon olive oil

1 small onion, finely chopped

200 g (7 oz) chestnut mushrooms, finely chopped

2 garlic cloves, sliced

4 tablespoons marsala

1 tablespoon fruit vinegar

2 tablespoons chopped coriander leaves

salt and pepper

1 If using frozen chicken livers, pat them dry on kitchen paper. Cut away any sinews and chop the livers into small pieces. Season with salt and pepper.

2 Melt half the butter with the oil in a large heavy-based frying pan. Add the livers and onion and fry quickly, stirring, for about 3 minutes until golden. Remove with a slotted spoon. Melt the remaining butter in the pan, add the mushrooms and garlic and cook, stirring, for 2 minutes.

3 Return the livers to the pan and add the marsala, vinegar and seasoning. Cover and cook gently for 3–4 minutes until the livers are still slightly pink in the centre. Add the coriander and serve.

Garlic, Parmesan and ciabatta sauce
This recipe provides a great use for ciabatta bread that's past its best, revitalized in a quick fry-up with olive oil, garlic, lemon, tomatoes and Parmesan.

PREPARATION TIME: 10 minutes

COOKING TIME: 3 minutes

SERVES: 4

150 g (5 oz) stale ciabatta

8 tablespoons extra virgin olive oil

2 garlic cloves, thinly sliced

finely grated rind and juice of 1 lemon

125 g (4 oz) sun-blush tomatoes, chopped

75 g (3 oz) Parmesan cheese, freshly grated

salt and pepper

1 Break the ciabatta into pieces, leaving the crust on, and blend lightly in a food processor to a very coarse crumb.

2 Heat half the oil in a frying pan. Add the breadcrumbs and garlic and fry gently for 1–2 minutes, stirring, until pale golden.

3 Add the lemon rind and juice, tomatoes, Parmesan, the remaining oil and plenty of salt and pepper. Heat through for 30 seconds, then serve.

Variations: This is a perfect recipe for using up any strongly flavoured ingredients that you might have left over. Try, for example, chopped anchovies, olives, capers, pine nuts or fresh herbs.

Fresh clam sauce
Fresh clams cooked in a tomato sauce help make up the Italian dish known as Spaghetti Vongole. You may have to cook this sauce on the spur of the moment as fresh clams, for most of us, are not very widely available.

PREPARATION TIME: 20 minutes

COOKING TIME: 20 minutes

SERVES: 4

1 kg (2 lb) small fresh clams

4 tablespoons olive oil

3 garlic cloves, crushed

¼ teaspoon crushed dried chillies

150 ml (¼ pint) dry white wine

2 x 400 g (13 oz) cans plum tomatoes

1 teaspoon caster sugar

small handful flat leaf parsley, chopped

finely grated rind and juice of ½ lemon

salt and pepper

1 Scrub the clams, discarding any damaged ones or open ones that do not close when tapped with a knife.

2 Heat the oil in a large heavy-based saucepan. Add the garlic and chillies and fry gently for 1 minute. Add the wine and let it bubble for 2 minutes, then add the tomatoes and sugar. Bring the sauce to the boil and cook for 8–10 minutes until it is thickened and pulpy, breaking up the tomatoes with a wooden spoon.

3 Tip the clams into the pan, cover with a lid and cook for 3–4 minutes until the clams have opened. Using a slotted spoon, lift about two-thirds of the clams out of the pan and remove them from their shells, discarding any shells that have not opened. Return the clams to the pan with the parsley, lemon rind and juice and salt and pepper. Heat through for 2 minutes and serve immediately.

Spicy sausage sauce

Packed with plenty of spices, this comforting sauce transforms even the dullest sausages into a deliciously meaty pasta topping. If you can get them, use sausages flavoured with apple, leek or mild spices which will work really well. Failing that, ordinary lean sausages will be fine.

PREPARATION TIME: 10 minutes

COOKING TIME: 20 minutes

SERVES: 4

2 teaspoons cardamom pods

1 teaspoon cumin seeds

1 teaspoon fennel seeds

2 tablespoons olive oil

1 red onion, thinly sliced

500 g (1 lb) sausages, skins removed

50 g (2 oz) pine nuts

3 tablespoons chopped herbs, such as parsley, fennel and coriander

150 g (5 oz) green cabbage, very finely shredded

300 ml (½ pint) single cream

salt and pepper

1 Crush the cardamom pods using a pestle and mortar to release the seeds. Discard the shells and add the cumin and fennel seeds. Crush until lightly ground.

2 Heat the oil in a large heavy-based frying pan and fry the onion for 3 minutes. Add the skinned sausages and fry gently, breaking the sausages up into small pieces with a wooden spoon, for 6–8 minutes until cooked through.

3 Add the pine nuts and crushed seeds to the pan and cook gently for 3–5 minutes, stirring frequently. Add the cabbage and fry for 2 minutes.

4 Pour in the cream and heat through for a further 2 minutes. Season with salt and pepper to taste and serve hot.

Spicy sausage sauce

Great with: *tagliatelle or macaroni*

When it comes to fish sauces, we're spoilt for choice. These sauces can be as varied in flavour, texture and colour as the extensive range of fish they're served with. We tend to think of fish sauces as being light and delicate but this is not always the case. Certainly some of the traditional flavours are here, such as tomato, watercress and saffron but stronger, meatier-flavoured fish can easily take a chunky, spicier sauce or one packed with nuts and garlic. Not everyone has a supply of good quality fresh fish, so bear in mind that it's often better to buy a reliable pack of frozen fish than fresh fish that's been on the slab too long. Whatever you decide on, the sauces in this chapter can be used to create meals that are perfect for both family suppers or special celebrations.

Rouille

This fiery Mediterranean sauce is traditionally served with fish soups and bouillabaisse. A quick and easy version can be made by beating finely crushed garlic and red chilli into ready-made mayonnaise, but this version, made with chargrilled red pepper, has extra flavour and colour.

PREPARATION TIME: 15 minutes, plus chilling

COOKING TIME: 10 minutes

SERVES: 6

1 large red pepper, deseeded

3 garlic cloves, roughly chopped

1 hot red chilli, deseeded and roughly chopped

1 egg yolk

25 g (1 oz) breadcrumbs

150 ml (¼ pint) olive oil

salt

1 Cut the pepper into thick strips. Heat a griddle until very hot, then add the pepper strips, skin-side down, and cook for about 15 minutes, turning frequently until the skin is blackened and charred. Alternatively, cook under a conventional grill. Leave to cool slightly, then peel away the skin.

2 Put the pepper into a food processor or blender with the garlic, chilli, egg yolk and a little salt and blend to a paste, scraping down the mixture from the sides of the bowl if necessary.

3 Add the breadcrumbs and 2 tablespoons of the oil and blend again to a paste.

4 Gradually pour in the remaining oil in a thin trickle, to make a sauce with a smooth consistency. Add a little more salt, if you like, then turn the sauce into a small serving dish. Cover and chill for up to 2 days before using.

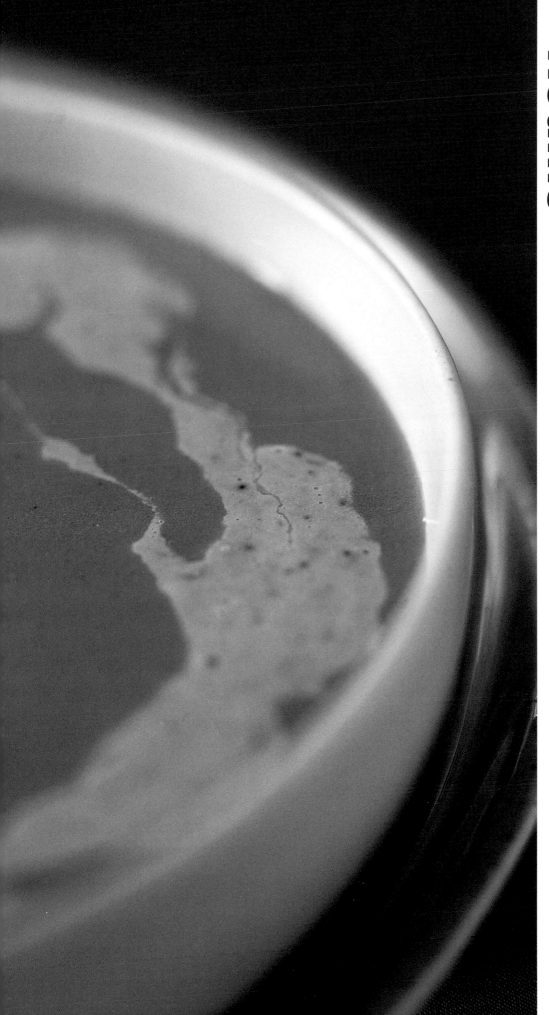

Rouille

Great with: *fish soups and stews, stirred in for a spicier flavour. Also good with barbecued or pan-fried fish*

Tomato coulis

A coulis is a sauce made from blended fruit or vegetable juice and is usually thin in consistency, with a clean, refreshing taste. Fresh tomatoes make a great coulis and if they are full of flavour, they will need few other additions. Like all coulis, this one looks stunning on white plates and topped with fish or vegetables.

PREPARATION TIME: 10 minutes

COOKING TIME: 14 minutes

SERVES: 4–6

750 g (1½ lb) tomatoes

4 tablespoons olive oil

2 garlic cloves, roughly chopped

2 shallots, chopped

several sprigs of thyme

½ teaspoon caster sugar

1 tablespoon tomato paste

salt and pepper

1 Skin the tomatoes (see page 9). Halve the tomatoes and scoop the seeds and pulp into a sieve set over a bowl to catch the juices. Using the back of a dessertspoon, press the pulp in the sieve to squeeze out as much of the juice as possible.

2 Heat the oil in a heavy-based saucepan and gently fry the garlic, shallots and thyme for 3 minutes until the shallots are soft.

3 Add the tomato flesh, sugar and a little salt and pepper. Cover the pan with a lid and simmer very gently for 10 minutes, stirring occasionally. Transfer the mixture to a food processor or blender and add the tomato juice and tomato paste. Blend until smooth. Serve warm or chilled.

Vegetable coulis

This delicious coulis can be used in the same way as tomato coulis but is best served hot. Serve it with tuna or shark steaks, or sea bass fillets.

PREPARATION TIME: 10 minutes

COOKING TIME: 20 minutes

SERVES: 6

25 g (1 oz) butter

2 tablespoons olive oil

1 small leek, trimmed and sliced

200 g (7 oz) courgettes, sliced

100 ml (3½ fl oz) white wine

75 g (3 oz) baby spinach

small handful of coriander or tarragon

1 tablespoon lemon juice

salt and pepper

1 Melt the butter with the oil in a heavy-based frying pan until bubbling. Add the leek and courgettes, cover with a lid or foil and cook very gently, stirring occasionally, until the vegetables are very tender but not browned, about 15 minutes.

2 Add the wine, spinach, coriander or tarragon and season with salt and pepper then bring to the boil. Cover and cook gently for 5 minutes.

3 Blend the mixture in a food processor or blender until very smooth. Return to the cleaned pan to reheat. Stir in the lemon juice, check the seasoning and serve hot.

Watercress sauce

A piece of beautifully cooked fish, bathed in a smooth, glossy, vibrantly coloured watercress sauce makes a really impressive main course. Watercress sauce is best served on the day it's made but if you want to get ahead, chill it and reheat it gently just before serving.

PREPARATION TIME: 5 minutes

COOKING TIME: 10 minutes

SERVES: 4

50 g (2 oz) butter

1 small onion, chopped

1 teaspoon plain flour

150 ml (¼ pint) **Vegetable Stock** (see page 12)

75 g (3 oz) watercress

3 tablespoons double cream

freshly grated nutmeg

salt and pepper

1 Melt the butter in a saucepan until bubbling. Add the onion and fry very gently for 5 minutes until softened but not browned. Add the flour and cook, stirring, for 1 minute.

2 Remove the pan from the heat and gradually blend in the stock, then add the watercress. (Don't bother to remove the stalks from the watercress.) Return the pan to the heat and bring just to the boil. Reduce the heat and simmer very gently for 2 minutes.

3 Transfer the mixture to a food processor or blender and blend until smooth. Return to the cleaned pan and add the cream, plenty of freshly grated nutmeg and salt and pepper. Heat through for 1 minute before serving.

Indian masala sauce

To make this sauce, you first prepare a spicy, gingery paste, then stir in the yogurt and stock and heat it through gently just before serving. If you want to make a small quantity of the sauce, you can keep the extra paste in the refrigerator for another time. It also goes well with chicken, pork or vegetable kebabs.

PREPARATION TIME: 10 minutes

COOKING TIME: 12 minutes

SERVES: 4

1 tablespoon cumin seeds

2 teaspoons fennel seeds

50 g (2 oz) fresh root ginger, peeled and roughly chopped

5 garlic cloves, roughly chopped

1 hot red or green chilli, deseeded and roughly chopped

2 tablespoons tomato paste

1 teaspoon ground turmeric

2 teaspoons caster sugar

4 tablespoons cold water

1 tablespoon vegetable oil

1 onion, finely chopped

150 ml (¼ pint) Chicken or Vegetable Stock (see page 12)

100 ml (3½ fl oz) natural yogurt

salt

1 Dry-fry the cumin and fennel seeds very gently in a small frying pan for 2 minutes until beginning to colour.

2 Tip the seeds into a food processor or blender and add the ginger, garlic, chilli, tomato paste, turmeric, sugar and cold water. Blend to a smooth paste, scraping the mixture down from the sides of the bowl if necessary.

3 Heat the oil in a frying pan and fry the onion for 5 minutes until lightly browned.

4 Add the spice paste, stock, yogurt and a little salt and bring slowly to the boil. Reduce the heat and simmer gently for 5 minutes until the sauce is thick and pulpy. Serve hot.

Prawn sauce

The great thing about this sauce is that even the shells aren't wasted; their colour and flavour add extra richness to the sauce. Combined with whole prawns and plenty of crème fraîche, it makes an indulgent treat for shellfish lovers.

PREPARATION TIME: 20 minutes

COOKING TIME: 30 minutes

SERVES: 4

500 g (1 lb) whole cooked prawns

40 g (1½ oz) butter

1 carrot, roughly chopped

2 celery sticks, roughly chopped

2 bay leaves

100 ml (3½ fl oz) white wine

400 ml (14 fl oz) water

2 tablespoons plain flour

¼ teaspoon cayenne pepper

100 ml (3½ fl oz) crème fraîche

salt and pepper

1 Peel the prawns, reserving the heads and shells. Melt 25 g (1 oz) of the butter in a large heavy-based saucepan until bubbling. Add the carrot, celery, bay leaves and prawn trimmings and fry gently for 4–5 minutes until just beginning to brown.

2 Add the wine and let it bubble for a few seconds. Add the water and bring to the boil. Reduce the heat, cover the pan and simmer gently for 20 minutes. Whizz the mixture in a food processor or blender to make a thin purée.

3 Strain the purée through a sieve into a bowl, pressing the pulp with the back of a dessertspoon.

4 Clean the pan, then melt the remaining butter. Add the flour and cook, stirring, for 1 minute. Off the heat, gradually blend in the strained fish stock, whisking well. Return to the heat and bring to the boil. Reduce the heat and add the cayenne pepper and crème fraîche. Simmer gently, stirring frequently, for 5 minutes until the sauce is thickened and smooth. Stir in the prawns, heat through gently for 30 seconds and serve hot.

Sauce vierge

This is an incredibly pretty, fresh-looking sauce that's easy to make but looks very impressive for summer entertaining. It uses plenty of olive oil so choose a good quality one for the best flavour. Mix the sauce a couple of hours in advance so it's ready to heat through gently before serving.

PREPARATION TIME: 10 minutes

COOKING TIME: 2 minutes

SERVES: 6

4 ripe tomatoes

½ teaspoon coriander seeds

15 g (½ oz) fresh herbs, such as chervil, flat leaf parsley, tarragon and chives

1 garlic clove, finely chopped

finely grated rind and juice of 1 lemon

100 ml (3½ fl oz) olive oil

salt and pepper

1 Skin the tomatoes (see page 9). Halve them and scoop out the seeds with a teaspoon. Chop the flesh into small dice.

2 Using a pestle and mortar, crush the coriander seeds as finely as possible. Discard the stalks from the herbs and finely chop the leaves.

3 In a bowl, mix together the diced tomatoes, coriander seeds, herbs, garlic, lemon rind and juice, and oil with a little salt and pepper. Cover and chill until ready to serve.

4 Tip the sauce into a small saucepan and heat through gently until hot.

Roasted garlic and almond sauce

This is a robust, punchy sauce that's lovely during the summer with salads and cold dishes that you can prepare ahead and leave in the refrigerator. Avocado oil, made from the first cold pressing of avocados, is delicious in dressings and sauces, but olive oil can be used as an alternative.

PREPARATION TIME: 5–10 minutes

COOKING TIME: 30 minutes

SERVES: 6

3 whole garlic bulbs

100 ml (3½ oz) avocado oil

1 slice white bread, crusts removed

50 g (2 oz) chopped almonds

50 g (2 oz) pine nuts

finely grated rind and juice of ½ lemon

salt and pepper

1 To roast the garlic, cut a thin slice off the top of each of the garlic bulbs. Place them on a piece of crumpled foil and drizzle with 1 tablespoon of the oil. Roast in a preheated oven, 200°C (400°F), Gas Mark 6, for about 30 minutes until the garlic feels soft when squeezed gently. Leave to cool slightly.

2 Meanwhile, put the bread into a small bowl and cover with cold water. Leave to soak for 5 minutes.

3 Squeeze the garlic flesh out of its skins into a food processor or blender. Lift the bread from the water and squeeze it dry. Add to the processor with the almonds, pine nuts and lemon rind and juice. Blend lightly until a paste forms.

4 With the machine running, gradually blend in the oil in a fine, steady trickle until the sauce is thick and smooth. Season to taste with salt and pepper and add a little more lemon juice for a tangier flavour, if you like. Transfer the sauce to a small serving bowl, cover and chill until ready to serve.

Dill and mustard sauce

This Swedish sauce is sweet but tangy and strongly flavoured with dill. It can be made ahead and keeps well in the refrigerator for several days. Serve it with hot or cold smoked fish, particularly salmon, or with a warm, new potato salad. Leftovers are delicious with salads or in cold meat sandwiches.

PREPARATION TIME: 10 minutes

SERVES: 8

15 g (½ oz) dill

2 tablespoons mild, wholegrain mustard

1 teaspoon Dijon mustard

2 tablespoons caster sugar

3 tablespoons white wine vinegar

150 ml (¼ pint) light olive oil

salt

1 Pull the dill from the sprigs and chop finely. Put the mustards, sugar and vinegar into a bowl and add a little salt.

2 Whisking constantly, gradually add the oil in a steady stream until the sauce is thick and smooth.

3 Stir in the dill and check the seasoning, adding a little more salt, vinegar or sugar, depending on personal preference.

Fennel and pancetta sauce

A quick and easy sauce that's delicious spooned over hot, steaming bowls of freshly cooked mussels, or with red mullet or sea bass.

PREPARATION TIME: 5 minutes

COOKING TIME: 15 minutes

SERVES: 4

25 g (1 oz) butter

1 large fennel bulb, trimmed and finely chopped

100 g (3½ oz) pancetta, finely chopped

100 ml (3½ fl oz) dry vermouth or medium dry white wine

150 ml (¼ pint) Fish Stock (see page 13)

1 egg yolk

150 ml (¼ pint) single cream

salt and pepper

1 Melt the butter in a heavy-based saucepan until bubbling. Add the fennel and pancetta and cook gently, stirring frequently, for 6–8 minutes until the fennel is very soft.

2 Pour in the vermouth or wine and let it bubble for a minute. Add the stock and a little salt and pepper and simmer gently for 5 minutes.

3 Blend the egg yolk and cream in a bowl and ladle in a little of the sauce. Tip the mixture back into the sauce and cook gently, stirring, until the sauce is slightly thickened. Check the seasoning and serve hot.

Thermidor sauce

Although traditionally served with lobster, this creamy sauce is good with almost any shellfish or white fish but, like all stock-based sauces, it's only worth making with really good quality fish stock. If you don't want to make your own, you can buy it fresh at some large supermarkets and good fishmongers.

PREPARATION TIME: 15 minutes

COOKING TIME: 25 minutes

SERVES: 6

400 ml (14 fl oz) Fish Stock (see page 13)

200 ml (7 fl oz) dry white wine

1 bouquet garni

15 g (½ oz) butter

15 g (½ oz) plain flour

300 ml (½ pint) full cream milk

2 teaspoons tomato paste

1 teaspoon English mustard

¼ teaspoon cayenne pepper

1 tablespoon finely chopped chervil or tarragon

150 ml (¼ pint) double cream

1 tablespoon brandy

salt

1 Put the fish stock, wine and bouquet garni into a large saucepan and bring to the boil. Cook until the stock has reduced to 200 ml (7 fl oz).

2 In a separate heavy-based saucepan, melt the butter until bubbling. Add the flour and cook, whisking, for 2 minutes until it is just beginning to colour. Remove from the heat and gradually blend in the milk, stirring until smooth. Return to the heat, add the tomato paste, mustard and cayenne and bring to the boil. Simmer for 5 minutes, stirring until thickened.

3 Remove the bouquet garni from the stock and pour the stock into the sauce.

4 Stir in the chervil or tarragon, cream and brandy and let the sauce bubble until it thinly coats the back of a wooden spoon. Check the seasoning and serve hot.

Thermidor sauce

Great with: *freshly cooked lobster and crab, or spooned over white fish fillets*

Chorizo and cherry tomato sauce

Adding pieces of spicy chorizo sausage to a tomato sauce is one of the easiest and tastiest ways of giving it plenty of bold flavour. This sauce is delicious with almost any white fish and with plain roast chicken.

PREPARATION TIME: 10 minutes

COOKING TIME: 15 minutes

SERVES: 4

3 tablespoons olive oil

1 large red onion, finely chopped

125 g (4 oz) piece chorizo sausage, skinned and finely diced

1 teaspoon fennel or celery seeds

400 g (13 oz) can cherry tomatoes

1 tablespoon wine vinegar

1 tablespoon clear honey

salt and pepper

1 Heat the oil in a saucepan. Add the onion and fry gently, stirring, for 3 minutes. Add the chorizo and fennel or celery seeds and fry for 2 minutes.

2 Strain the cherry tomatoes through a sieve into the pan, reserving the whole pieces. Add the vinegar, honey and a little salt and pepper to the pan and bring to the boil. Reduce the heat, cover with a lid and cook very gently for 8 minutes.

3 Add the strained tomatoes and check the seasoning. Heat through for 1 minute and serve hot.

Saffron cream sauce *This rich, velvety sauce is thickened with cream. For best results use a well-flavoured, homemade fish stock or a good quality, ready-made one. Serve the sauce spooned over portions of plated fish, with shellfish or toss with fish and fresh pasta.*

PREPARATION TIME: 5 minutes

COOKING TIME: 15 minutes

SERVES: 4

15 g (½ oz) butter

1 tablespoon plain flour

300 ml (½ pint) Fish Stock (see page 13)

½ teaspoon saffron threads

2 teaspoons lemon juice

75 ml (3 fl oz) double cream

salt and pepper

1 Melt the butter in a heavy-based saucepan until bubbling. Add the flour and cook, stirring continuously with a wooden spoon, for 2 minutes, or until it starts to turn golden.

2 Remove the pan from the heat and gradually blend in the fish stock, stirring until smooth.

3 Sprinkle in the saffron threads, crushing them between your finger and thumb. Squeeze in the lemon juice. Return to the heat and bring just to the boil, stirring. Reduce the heat and gently simmer the sauce for 5 minutes, stirring occasionally, until it is slightly thickened and smooth.

4 Stir in the cream and cook for a further 5 minutes until the sauce thinly coats the back of a wooden spoon. Season to taste with salt and pepper and serve hot.

Variation: Add 2–3 tablespoons dry vermouth with the cream.

Honey, balsamic vinegar and mushroom sauce

The honey and balsamic vinegar give the sautéed mushrooms an inviting sheen in this simple sauce. Sweet and tangy, it's particularly good with oily fish such as salmon, trout, mackerel or herrings.

PREPARATION TIME: 5 minutes

COOKING TIME: 8 minutes

SERVES: 4

200 g (7 oz) shiitake mushrooms

2 tablespoons sunflower oil

1 tablespoon lemon juice

several sprigs of thyme

2 tablespoons clear honey

4 tablespoons balsamic vinegar

2 tablespoons chopped chives

salt and pepper

1 Cut up any large mushrooms, so they're all about the same size. Heat the oil in a frying pan and gently fry the mushrooms for 5 minutes, stirring. Remove the pan from the heat.

2 Add the lemon juice, thyme, honey and vinegar, and cook gently, stirring, for 2 minutes until the sauce is heated through and syrupy.

3 Stir in the chives and a little salt and pepper and cook for 1 minute more. Serve hot.

Tarragon cream sauce

This sauce uses the same method as Béchamel Sauce, but the roux is cooked a little longer and stock is used instead of milk. The result, a Velouté Sauce, can be served as it is or given extra zip with herbs and other flavourings, as it is here.

PREPARATION TIME: 10 minutes

COOKING TIME: 15 minutes

SERVES: 6

25 g (1 oz) butter

25 g (1 oz) plain flour

500 ml (17 fl oz) **Fish Stock** (see page 13)

8 large tarragon sprigs

150 ml (¼ pint) dry white wine

½ teaspoon medium curry paste

4 tablespoons crème fraîche or single cream

salt and pepper

1 Melt the butter in a heavy-based saucepan until bubbling. Tip in the flour and cook gently, stirring with a wooden spoon, for 3–4 minutes until the roux is golden brown.

2 Remove the pan from the heat and gradually blend in the fish stock, stirring until smooth. Return the pan to the heat and bring to the boil, stirring. Reduce the heat and simmer gently, stirring until the sauce thinly coats the back of a wooden spoon.

3 Pull the tarragon leaves from the stalks and roughly chop the leaves.

4 Add the tarragon to the sauce with the wine, curry paste, crème fraîche and a little salt and pepper and let the sauce bubble for about 5 minutes until smooth and glossy. Serve hot.

Tarragon cream sauce

Great with: *Steamed mussels, salmon, trout or firm white fish*

When we think of sauces to serve with meat, we think of all the classic, traditional combinations such as tangy fruity sauces with fatty meats and creamy smooth ones with lean meats. This is a good starting point when planning a menu but isn't essential. Apple sauce is good with pork, horseradish with beef and mint with lamb, but there's a fabulous choice of other classic and modern sauces using fruit, spices, herbs and alcohol. When making sauces for meat, don't forget that the delicious juices that accumulate during roasting or pan-frying can be added to the sauce for extra flavour. Many of these sauces keep well in the refrigerator and can be served with cold cuts during the week or used to add extra interest to sandwiches and snacks.

Spicy damson sauce

A smaller variety of plum, damsons have a tart flavour and are most often used in preserves and jellies. Their season is relatively short so it's well worth buying some and freezing them for later. If you can't get damsons for this sauce, use firm, tart plums instead.

PREPARATION TIME: 10 minutes

COOKING TIME: 12 minutes

SERVES: 4

250 g (8 oz) damsons

1 shallot, finely chopped

4 tablespoons water

finely grated rind and juice of 1 lime

50 g (2 oz) light muscovado sugar

½ teaspoon five-spice powder

1 Score each damson with a knife and put them into a heavy-based saucepan with the shallot and water.

2 Cover the pan with a lid and cook very gently for 10 minutes until the damsons are very soft, breaking them up with a wooden spoon.

3 Turn the mixture into a sieve set over a clean pan and press the pulp with the back of a dessertspoon to extract as much juice as possible. Don't forget to scrape the pulp from under the sieve into the pan.

4 Add the lime rind and juice, sugar and five-spice powder and heat through very gently until the sugar has dissolved and the sauce is smooth and glossy, about 2 minutes. Check that the sauce is sweet enough. It should be tangy but not too sharp. Add a little extra sugar if necessary. Serve warm or cold.

Spicy damson sauce

Great with: *pork and lamb chops, duck breasts and venison, or for stirring into casseroles or gravies*

Cumberland sauce

This is a versatile sauce that's as good with rich, fatty meats as it is with cold meats, pâtés and pork pies and tastes as good cold as it does hot. It will keep in the refrigerator for several days and reheats well.

PREPARATION TIME: 10 minutes

COOKING TIME: 15 minutes

SERVES: 4

1 orange

1 lemon

1 shallot, finely chopped

2 tablespoons red wine vinegar

150 ml (¼ pint) Beef or Chicken Stock
(see pages 10 and 12)

75 ml (3 fl oz) port

5 tablespoons redcurrant jelly

good pinch of cayenne pepper

salt

1 Using a small, sharp knife, pare the rind from half the orange and cut it into fine shreds. Blanch them in a pan of boiling water for 1 minute. Drain.

2 Squeeze the juice from the orange and the lemon and put it into a small heavy-based saucepan with the shallot, vinegar, stock, port, redcurrant jelly, cayenne pepper and a little salt. Bring to the boil, then reduce the heat and simmer gently for about 10 minutes until the jelly has melted and the sauce is turning syrupy.

3 Add the orange shreds and cook gently for 2 minutes. Serve warm or cold.

Red wine gravy

The rich, caramelized juices from a large roast joint of beef, lamb or pork provide the base for a deliciously well-flavoured gravy that can turn a plain roast into something far more tasty. Some sliced onion, garlic and herb sprigs, placed under the meat for roasting, will enhance the finished flavour.

PREPARATION TIME: 5 minutes

COOKING TIME: 5 minutes

SERVES: 6

pan juices from roasted meat

2 teaspoons plain flour

300 ml (½ pint) Beef or Lamb Stock
(see page 10)

150 ml (¼ pint) full-bodied red wine

salt and pepper

1 Tilt the roasting tin with the pan juices and skim off the fat from the surface with a large metal spoon. Add the flour to the pan and cook over a moderate heat for 1 minute, stirring.

2 Add the stock, wine and salt and pepper and bring to the boil. Reduce the heat and cook gently, stirring to scrape up the residue in the pan until the gravy is slightly thickened and glossy. Check the seasoning and strain into a jug.

Variations: To make a chicken gravy, use chicken stock and white wine instead of the red. Other flavourings such as ground cumin or coriander and redcurrant jelly can be added to a lamb gravy. Mustard or horseradish sauce is good with beef.

Pear, prune and cider sauce
This tangy sauce uses ingredients from the storecupboard and provides a delicious contrast to bacon and gammon. It can also be served chilled with pâtés, terrines, cold meat and game. Because of its chutney-like quality, it can be stored for up to 2 weeks.

PREPARATION TIME: 10 minutes

COOKING TIME: 35 minutes

SERVES: 6

1 tablespoon sunflower oil

1 small onion, finely chopped

100 g (3½ oz) dried pears, finely chopped

100 g (3½ oz) prunes, finely chopped

450 ml (¾ pint) medium cider

½ teaspoon ground allspice

1 tablespoon light muscovado sugar

2 tablespoons fruit vinegar

salt and pepper

1 Heat the oil in a heavy-based saucepan, add the onion and fry gently for 3 minutes. Add the pears, prunes, cider, allspice, sugar and vinegar, season with salt and pepper, and bring slowly to the boil.

2 Reduce the heat and simmer very gently for about 30 minutes, or until the fruits are soft and the sauce is turning pulpy, stirring occasionally. Check the seasoning.

3 For a smooth sauce, blend the ingredients in a food processor or blender to a purée. Serve the sauce warm or chilled.

Variation: For a spicier flavour, try adding a small piece of finely chopped fresh root ginger or ½ teaspoon five-spice powder.

Beer and onion sauce

Sausages and mash wouldn't be the same without this comforting golden sauce. Give the onions plenty of time to fry gently in the butter so their flavour will be sweet and mellow. If you don't want to use beer, simply replace it with more stock, although beer gives the sauce a lovely flavour and tang.

PREPARATION TIME: 10 minutes

COOKING TIME: 25 minutes

SERVES: 4

25 g (1 oz) butter

1 tablespoon vegetable oil

several sprigs of thyme

8 sage leaves, shredded

500 g (1 lb) onions, chopped

1 teaspoon caster sugar

2 garlic cloves, crushed

1 tablespoon plain flour

150 ml (¼ pint) Beef, Chicken or Vegetable Stock (see pages 10 and 12)

300 ml (½ pint) beer

salt and pepper

1 Melt the butter with the oil in a heavy-based frying pan. Pull the thyme leaves from the stalks and add them to the pan with the sage, onions and sugar.

2 Cover the pan and cook very gently for about 15 minutes until the onions are very tender and lightly coloured, stirring frequently.

3 Add the garlic and raise the temperature. Fry the mixture, uncovered, for 3 minutes, or until deep golden. Add the flour and cook, stirring, for 1 minute.

4 Add the stock, beer and a little salt and pepper. Bring to the boil, then reduce the heat and cook gently for 5 minutes until the sauce is glossy and slightly thickened. Season to taste with salt and pepper and serve hot.

Beer and onion sauce

Great with: *sausages and mash, liver and bacon or meat pie*

Leek and nutmeg sauce

This lovely, creamy sauce really brings out the colour and flavour of the leeks. It goes particularly well with lamb, pan-fried lambs' liver and with baked ham. It's flavoured at the end of the cooking process with a blend of cream and egg yolks, which thicken and enrich the sauce.

PREPARATION TIME: 10 minutes

COOKING TIME: 15 minutes

SERVES: 6

25 g (1 oz) butter

1 tablespoon olive oil

1 small onion, finely chopped

250 g (8 oz) small leeks, trimmed and chopped

2 bay leaves

300 ml (½ pint) Vegetable or Chicken Stock (see page 12)

plenty of freshly grated nutmeg

2 egg yolks

150 ml (¼ pint) single cream

salt and pepper

1 Melt the butter with the oil in a heavy-based saucepan. Add the onion, leeks and bay leaves and cook gently, stirring frequently, until the vegetables are quite soft, about 6–8 minutes.

2 Add the stock and bring to the boil. Reduce the heat, add the nutmeg and simmer the sauce, covered with a lid, for 5 minutes.

3 Blend the egg yolks with the cream in a small bowl and stir in a ladleful of the sauce. Tip the mixture back into the pan and heat the sauce very gently, stirring until thickened. Season to taste with salt and pepper and serve hot.

Peppercorn sauce

This creamy, blended peppercorn sauce is delicious with any well-seasoned, pan-fried, lean, tender beef steak or lamb chop. Or, of course, you can grill if you want a lighter alternative. If you are frying the meat, finish the sauce in the pan so it absorbs all the flavoured cooking juices.

PREPARATION TIME: 5 minutes

COOKING TIME: 8 minutes

SERVES: 4

2 tablespoons green peppercorns in brine, drained

25 g (1 oz) butter

1 small onion, finely chopped

2 garlic cloves, finely chopped

200 ml (7 fl oz) crème fraîche

2 tablespoons finely chopped parsley

salt

1 Crush the peppercorns fairly finely using a pestle and mortar. Melt the butter in a frying pan until bubbling and gently fry the onion for 5 minutes until soft. Add the garlic and fry for a further minute.

2 Tip the peppercorns into the pan with the crème fraîche, parsley and a little salt. Heat through gently for 2 minutes before serving.

Apple sauce
A classic accompaniment to roast pork and goose, apple sauce is also delicious with chicken, lamb, duck, game and other rich, fatty meats. Leftover sauce is great in warm sandwiches or in baguettes with cold meats. The secret of a good apple sauce is to use plenty of butter and let the apples and flavourings cook very slowly.

PREPARATION TIME: 10 minutes

COOKING TIME: 20 minutes

SERVES: 6

50 g (2 oz) butter

3 large cooking apples, peeled, cored and chopped

50 g (2 oz) caster sugar

6 whole cloves

finely grated rind and juice of 1 lemon

salt

1 Melt the butter in a heavy-based saucepan. Add the apples, sugar, cloves, lemon rind and juice and a little salt.

2 Cover the pan with a lid and leave to cook gently over the lowest heat for about 20 minutes, stirring the mixture occasionally, until the apples are very soft and mushy. Check the seasoning, adding a little more lemon juice, if you like, for a tangier flavour. Transfer to a sauce boat and serve warm or cold.

Variation: For a smooth apple sauce, use ¼ teaspoon ground cloves instead of the whole ones and whizz to a purée in a food processor or blender.

Mint sauce
This classic sauce goes with pan-fried duck breasts as well as grilled and roast lamb. Don't throw away any leftover mint sauce after a lamb dinner – add a splash of olive oil and serve it as a dressing for warm new potatoes or drizzle over peas or mangetout.

PREPARATION TIME: 10 minutes, plus infusing

SERVES: 6

15 g (½ oz) mint

1 tablespoon caster sugar

1 tablespoon boiling water

2 tablespoons white wine vinegar

1 Pull the mint leaves from their stalks and chop them finely.

2 Put the mint into a small bowl with the sugar and the boiling water. Leave to infuse for 5 minutes, stirring once or twice until the sugar dissolves.

3 Add the vinegar and leave to stand for about 1 hour before serving.

Satay sauce

This is deliciously rich, spicy and peanutty and serves several different purposes. It is generally used as a main meal accompaniment, but it's also good as a dipping sauce, served on a platter with a selection of vegetables or small pieces of skewered chicken, pork or fish.

PREPARATION TIME: 10 minutes

COOKING TIME: 7 minutes

SERVES: 4–6

1 lemongrass stalk

1 small onion, chopped

2 garlic cloves, chopped

1 teaspoon shrimp paste or Thai fish sauce

1 teaspoon tamarind paste

1 hot red chilli, deseeded and chopped

2 tablespoons water

1 tablespoon light muscovado sugar

200 ml (7 fl oz) coconut milk

175 g (6 oz) smooth or crunchy peanut butter

1 tablespoon soy sauce

1 Trim the ends from the lemongrass and remove any coarse or damaged outer leaves. Cut the lemongrass into thin slices.

2 Put the lemongrass, onion, garlic, shrimp paste or fish sauce, tamarind paste and chilli into a food processor or blender. Add the water and sugar and blend to a paste, scraping down the mixture from the sides of the bowl if necessary.

3 Transfer the mixture to a saucepan with the coconut milk. Bring almost to the boil (watching closely so the coconut milk does not boil over), then reduce the heat and simmer very gently for 5 minutes.

4 Add the peanut butter and soy sauce and cook very gently for 2 minutes, or until the sauce is heated through and thickened. Check the seasoning, adding a dash more soy sauce, if you like, and more coconut milk if the sauce is too thick. Transfer to a serving bowl and serve warm.

Satay sauce

Great with: *lean pork or chicken kebabs, or steak. Satay sauce also makes an excellent dip for crudités or a dressing for Gado Gado, a beansprout and vegetable salad*

Redcurrant and ginger sauce

Fruity sauces provide a delicious contrast to the rich flavour and fattiness of some meats. This recipe is mildly gingery and very fresh and light, making it perfect for summer eating. It goes particularly well with roast or grilled lamb, duck or game and can be served warm or cold.

PREPARATION TIME: 10 minutes

COOKING TIME: 8 minutes

SERVES: 4

200 g (7 oz) fresh or frozen redcurrants

1 shallot, grated

15 g (½ oz) fresh root ginger, peeled and grated

6 tablespoons water

½ teaspoon cornflour

1 tablespoon redcurrant jelly

2 teaspoons red wine vinegar

1 Remove the redcurrants from their stalks by running them through the tines of a fork. Reserve half and put the remainder in a small frying pan with the grated shallot, ginger and 4 tablespoons of the water. Heat gently for 2–3 minutes until the juices run and start to bubble.

2 Blend the cornflour with the remaining water and add to the pan with the redcurrant jelly and red wine vinegar.

3 Heat gently, stirring, until the jelly has melted and the sauce is slightly thickened. Stir in the reserved redcurrants and heat through very gently for 1 minute before serving.

Normandy apple sauce

The combination of apples, mustard and cream is a classic Norman one, traditionally served with grilled or roasted meat, particularly pork and chicken.

PREPARATION TIME: 10 minutes

COOKING TIME: 25 minutes

SERVES: 5–6

25 g (1 oz) butter

1 small onion, finely chopped

2 crisp dessert apples, peeled, cored and roughly chopped

300 ml (½ pint) Chicken Stock (see page 12)

2 tablespoons Calvados or brandy (optional)

6 tarragon sprigs, leaves removed and roughly chopped

3 tablespoons crème fraîche

1 tablespoon wholegrain mustard

1 teaspoon Dijon mustard

salt and pepper

1 Melt the butter in a heavy-based saucepan until bubbling. Add the onion and fry gently until softened. Add the apples and cook for 5 minutes until softened and just beginning to colour.

2 Stir in the stock and Calvados or brandy, if using. Bring to the boil, then reduce the heat and simmer very gently, covered, for 10 minutes. Transfer the mixture to a food processor or blender and blend until smooth. Strain through a sieve back into the cleaned pan.

3 Add the tarragon to the pan with the crème fraîche, both mustards and a little salt and pepper. Heat through gently for 5 minutes and serve hot.

Horseradish sauce

Fresh horseradish has a fiery freshness and keeps well in the refrigerator. It can be grated finely into mayonnaise or yogurt as a salad dressing or into meat or vegetable stews to add a bit of bite. Horseradish sauce is most often served with roast beef but also tastes good with baked or pan-fried cod, salmon or skate.

PREPARATION TIME: 5 minutes

SERVES: 6

small length fresh horseradish root
1 teaspoon caster sugar
1 tablespoon white wine vinegar
150 ml (¼ pint) double cream
salt

1 Peel the horseradish using a vegetable peeler and finely grate the root until you have about 4 tablespoons. Put the grated root into a bowl with the sugar and vinegar and stir until the sugar has dissolved.

2 Add the cream and a pinch of salt and whisk with a balloon whisk or hand-held electric whisk until the mixture just starts to hold its shape. (The flavour of horseradish root varies in intensity so check that it's strong enough; if necessary, grate in a little more.)

3 Transfer the sauce to a serving dish and chill, loosely covered, until you are ready to serve.

Variation: For a sweeter horseradish sauce, reduce the vinegar to 1–2 teaspoons and double the sugar.

Of all the sauce partners, chicken is perhaps the most versatile. Like fish, it makes a great marriage with delicate flavours such as lemon, tarragon, chervil and tomatoes, yet it is meaty enough to take the robust spiciness of a Devilled Tomato or aromatic Thai Green Curry Sauce. Prepare the chicken in a way that complements the sauce; for example, a light glossy mushroom sauce works well with poached or pan-fried chicken breasts while a curried sauce can take the richer, oilier flavour of a garlicky roasted chicken. Don't forget all the less obvious choices of poultry and game. Served with Creamy Bread Sauce, smoky Walnut Sauce or tangy Quince and Juniper Sauce, meats such as turkey, pheasant, duck, goose or pigeon can be enjoyed well beyond the festive season.

Sauces for poultry and game

Griddled aubergine sauce

This unusual sauce is mildly spiced without being overpowering, but if you want a hotter flavour, add a finely chopped red or green chilli. Make sure the aubergines are well and truly charred to give the sauce plenty of colour and flavour.

PREPARATION TIME: 15 minutes

COOKING TIME: 30 minutes

SERVES: 6–8

½ **teaspoon celery salt**

1 **teaspoon mild chilli powder**

400 g (13 oz) **aubergines, sliced lengthways**

6 **tablespoons sunflower oil**

1 **large red onion, chopped**

3 **garlic cloves, chopped**

1 **tablespoon black onion seeds**

1 **teaspoon ground fenugreek**

6–8 **large mint leaves, chopped**

150 ml (¼ pint) **Vegetable Stock** (see page 12)

3 **tablespoons sun-dried tomato paste**

100 ml (3½ fl oz) **crème fraîche**

1 Heat a griddle. Mix together the celery salt and chilli powder and rub over the aubergine slices. Brush one side of each slice with a little oil. Lay several slices, oiled-sides down, on the griddle. You'll need to cook them in batches.

2 Cook the aubergine slices until charred, about 6 minutes. Turn them over, brush with more oil and cook until very soft.

3 Heat the remaining oil in a large frying pan. Add the onion and garlic and fry gently for 3 minutes. Add the black onion seeds, fenugreek and mint, and fry for a further 2 minutes. Tip the onion mixture into a food processor or blender. Add the aubergine slices and blend to a slightly chunky paste.

4 Turn the mixture into a cleaned pan and add the stock and tomato paste. Heat through gently, stirring. Swirl in the crème fraîche and serve.

Griddled aubergine sauce

Great with: *roast chicken or chicken portions, turkey or guinea fowl*

Devilled tomato sauce
The simplest roast chicken can be transformed into a far more interesting dish with this spicy, tangy accompaniment.

PREPARATION TIME: 15 minutes

COOKING TIME: 20 minutes

SERVES: 6

500 g (1 lb) tomatoes

25 g (1 oz) butter

1 small onion, chopped

2 garlic cloves, crushed

1 tablespoon Worcestershire sauce

2 tablespoons wholegrain mustard

finely grated rind and juice of 1 lemon

several sprigs of thyme

3 tablespoons mango chutney

salt and pepper

soured cream, to serve

1 Skin the tomatoes (see page 9).

2 Melt the butter in a large saucepan until bubbling. Add the onion and fry gently for 3 minutes until softened. Stir in the garlic, Worcestershire sauce, mustard, lemon rind and juice, thyme, chopped tomatoes, mango chutney and a little salt and pepper.

3 Cook gently for 15 minutes until the mixture is thick and pulpy, breaking up any large pieces of tomato with a wooden spoon. Remove the thyme sprigs and check the seasoning. Serve hot topped with spoonfuls of soured cream.

Creamy bread sauce
This much neglected sauce is ideal with a simple Sunday roast and uses ingredients from the storecupboard. Those who dislike the distinctive flavour of cloves can leave them out. In this case, chop the onions and soften them in the butter before finishing the sauce.

PREPARATION TIME: 10 minutes

COOKING TIME: 15 minutes

SERVES: 8

2 onions

8 cloves

450 ml (¾ pint) full cream milk

2 bay leaves

150 g (5 oz) fresh white breadcrumbs

25 g (1 oz) butter

1 tablespoon green peppercorns in brine, drained and lightly crushed

freshly grated nutmeg

3 tablespoons double cream

salt

1 Peel the onions but leave them whole and stud with the cloves. Put them in a saucepan with the milk and bay leaves and bring the milk almost to the boil, then reduce the heat and cook on the lowest setting for 10 minutes to let the flavours infuse.

2 Remove the onions from the sauce and add the breadcrumbs, butter, peppercorns and plenty of freshly grated nutmeg. Cook gently for 5 minutes until the sauce is thick and pulpy.

3 Stir in the cream and season with salt and pepper to taste. Serve hot sprinkled with extra grated nutmeg.

Walnut sauce
In some Mediterranean countries and in the Middle East, whole nuts are used as the base of sauces to accompany meat, chicken and fish dishes. The sauces are never completely smooth, but the flavour is delicious, particularly with the addition of garlic and spices.

PREPARATION TIME: 15 minutes

COOKING TIME: 10 minutes

SERVES: 6

2 tablespoons walnut oil

2 shallots, chopped

275 g (9 oz) walnut halves

2 slices white bread, crusts removed

450–500 ml (15–17 fl oz) Chicken Stock
(see page 12)

2 teaspoons smoked paprika

3 garlic cloves, roughly chopped

salt

1 Heat the oil in a small saucepan and fry the shallots gently for 3 minutes, or until softened. Lightly toast 25 g (1 oz) of the walnut halves, chop them roughly and set aside.

2 Tear the bread into small pieces and put it into a bowl with 100 ml (3½ fl oz) of the stock. Leave for 5 minutes.

3 Tip the remaining walnuts into a food processor or blender and blend until finely ground. Add the bread with the soaking liquid, the shallots and oil, paprika and garlic, and blend until smooth, then gradually blend in another 350 ml (12 fl oz) of the stock.

4 Turn the sauce into a saucepan and heat gently for 3–5 minutes until hot, adding a little more stock if necessary to make a thick sauce. Season to taste and serve hot.

Variation: Smoked paprika is not essential in this sauce, but it does add a really delicious flavour and warm colour to it. Alternatively, use ordinary paprika and some black pepper.

Black bean sauce

Salted black beans are available in bags or jars from Asian supermarkets. They're spiced and fermented and you will find that a little goes a long way in this sweet, tangy sauce. Don't be tempted to use ordinary, canned or dried black beans as they have a totally different flavour.

PREPARATION TIME: 15 minutes

COOKING TIME: 8 minutes

SERVES: 4

1 teaspoon cornflour

150 ml (¼ pint) **Chicken Stock** (see page 12)

2 tablespoons sesame oil

1 tablespoon seasoned rice wine vinegar

1 red chilli, deseeded and finely chopped

1 tablespoon soy sauce

2 tablespoons salted black beans

2 tablespoons vegetable oil

2 garlic cloves

15 g (½ oz) fresh root ginger, peeled and finely chopped

½ bunch of spring onions, finely chopped

1 small green pepper, deseeded and finely sliced

1 tablespoon sesame seeds

1 Put the cornflour into a small bowl and gradually blend in the stock. Add the sesame oil, rice wine vinegar, chilli and soy sauce.

2 Rinse the black beans under running cold water. Heat the oil in a large frying pan or wok. Add the black beans, garlic, ginger, spring onions and green pepper and cook, stirring constantly, for 3–4 minutes until the vegetables are just beginning to colour.

3 Remove the pan from the heat and tip in the blended sauce and the sesame seeds.

4 Return the pan to the heat and cook very gently, stirring frequently, until the sauce is thickened and glossy. Check the seasoning, adding a little more soy sauce if liked. Serve hot.

Black bean sauce

Great with: *stir-fried chicken, turkey or duck. It's also good with stir-fried steak, vegetables or steamed whole fish*

Tarragon and mustard seed sauce

A lovely, tangy sauce that's delicious with cold cuts of chicken, turkey or game, particularly those left from a roast dinner.

PREPARATION TIME: 5 minutes, plus chilling

COOKING TIME: 3–4 minutes

SERVES: 4

1 tablespoon black or white mustard seeds

6 large tarragon sprigs

finely grated rind and juice of 1 lime

1 teaspoon English mustard

2 spring onions, trimmed and roughly chopped

2 garlic cloves, roughly chopped

2 teaspoons caster sugar

100 ml (3½ fl oz) sunflower oil or light olive oil

salt

1 Dry-fry the mustard seeds in a small frying pan for 3–4 minutes until the seeds start to pop. Pull the tarragon leaves from the stalks and put them into a food processor or blender with the mustard seeds.

2 Add the lime rind and juice, mustard, spring onions, garlic, sugar and a little salt and blend until smooth, scraping the mixture down from the sides of the bowl if necessary.

3 With the machine running, gradually blend in the oil until the sauce is thick and smooth. Turn into a small serving dish, cover and chill until ready to serve.

Quince and juniper sauce
Fresh quinces are quite difficult to buy, so this sauce is definitely one to make if you, or a friend or neighbour, have a quince tree in the garden. It makes a delicious combination with the distinctive, gin-like flavour of the juniper – so good with poultry and game dishes.

PREPARATION TIME: 15 minutes

COOKING TIME: 20 minutes

SERVES: 4–6

2 teaspoons juniper berries

500 g (1 lb) fresh quinces

4 tablespoons water

25 g (1 oz) golden caster sugar

finely grated rind and juice of ½ lemon

1 Crush the juniper berries using a pestle and mortar or a small bowl and the end of a rolling pin.

2 Peel and core the quinces and put them into a heavy-based saucepan with the crushed berries and the water.

3 Cover the pan with a lid and cook gently for about 20 minutes until the fruit is very soft and pulpy. Strain the fruit through a sieve into a cleaned pan, pressing the pulp in the sieve with the back of a dessertspoon to extract as much fruit as possible.

4 Stir in the sugar and lemon rind and juice, then heat through gently until the sugar dissolves. Serve warm or cold.

Pumpkin and rosemary sauce *Like most pumpkin recipes, it's the addition of aromatic herbs or spices that gives this sauce a punchy flavour. Fresh rosemary adds a warm, earthy flavour while the ginger and chilli stop the pumpkin tasting bland. Serve it with roast turkey or chicken, pork chops or gammon steaks.*

PREPARATION TIME: 15 minutes

COOKING TIME: 25 minutes

SERVES: 6

500 g (1 lb) wedge pumpkin, deseeded

25 g (1 oz) butter

1 onion, chopped

4 large sprigs of rosemary

2 garlic cloves, roughly chopped

¼ teaspoon crushed dried chillies

100 ml (3½ fl oz) dry white wine

250 ml (8 fl oz) Vegetable or Chicken Stock
(see page 12)

1 piece stem ginger from a jar, finely chopped

3 tablespoons crème fraîche

salt and pepper

1 Cut away the skin from the pumpkin and cut the flesh into chunks. Melt the butter in a large saucepan until bubbling. Add the onion and fry gently for 3 minutes until softened.

2 Add the pumpkin to the pan with the rosemary sprigs, garlic and chillies, and cook for 5 minutes, stirring frequently, until just beginning to colour. Add the wine, stock and ginger, and bring to the boil. Reduce the heat, cover the pan and simmer gently for 15 minutes until the pumpkin is tender.

3 Lift out the rosemary sprigs and blend the mixture to a smooth sauce, either in a food processor or using a hand-held electric blender. Whisk in the crème fraîche and season with salt and pepper to taste. Reheat gently and serve.

Thai green sauce

With their unique depth of flavour but fresh, light taste, it's easy to see why Thai-style curries have become so popular. The blended paste keeps well in the refrigerator so you could make up a double batch and keep half for the following week.

PREPARATION TIME: 10 minutes

COOKING TIME: 25 minutes

SERVES: 4

2 lemongrass stalks, trimmed and sliced

50 g (2 oz) piece fresh root ginger, peeled and roughly chopped

4 garlic cloves, roughly chopped

1 onion, roughly chopped

2 hot green chillies, deseeded and chopped

large bunch of coriander, about 25 g (1 oz)

½ teaspoon ground turmeric

1 teaspoon ground cumin

2 tablespoons water

1 tablespoon caster sugar

1 tablespoon Thai fish sauce

1 tablespoon lime juice

400 ml (14 fl oz) can coconut milk

salt

1 Put the lemongrass into a food processor and add the ginger, garlic, onion, chillies, coriander, turmeric and cumin. Add the water and blend to a fairly fine paste.

2 Stir in the caster sugar, fish sauce and lime juice, then turn the mixture into a bowl if you are not using it immediately. Cover and chill.

3 Put the coconut milk into a heavy-based saucepan. Bring to the boil and cook for 10–15 minutes, until it has reduced by about a third and has thickened enough to coat a spoon very thinly.

4 Tip the curry paste into the pan and whisk into the coconut milk. Reduce the heat to its lowest setting and cook the sauce very gently, covered, for 10 minutes. Season with salt and serve hot.

Thai green sauce

Great with: *baked or pan-fried chicken breasts, prawns or vegetable noodles. Or, add diced raw chicken to the sauce at step 4*

Cranberry, cinnamon and orange sauce

Even if you only eat cranberry sauce once a year, it's worth making your own. As well as going perfectly with roast turkey, baked game or duck, this sauce is delicious in sandwiches and with cold meats.

PREPARATION TIME: 5 minutes

COOKING TIME: 15 minutes

SERVES: 8–10

250 g (8 oz) fresh or frozen cranberries

1 cinnamon stick

finely grated rind and juice of 1 large orange

3 tablespoons orange marmalade

50 g (2 oz) light muscovado sugar

50 ml (2 fl oz) water

50 ml (2 fl oz) Cointreau or other orange-flavoured liqueur

1 Tip the cranberries into a saucepan and add the cinnamon stick, orange rind and juice, orange marmalade, sugar and water.

2 Heat gently, stirring, until the sugar and marmalade have dissolved, then let the sauce simmer for about 15 minutes, stirring occasionally, until the cranberries have burst and the sauce has thickened slightly. (It will thicken more as it cools.)

3 Leave the sauce to cool completely, then remove the cinnamon stick. Cover the sauce and chill until ready to serve.

Variations: Try some freshly grated ginger or a little allspice instead of the cinnamon. Port is often used instead of the orange liqueur or you can leave out the alcohol altogether and use extra fruit juice.

Red bean and okra sauce

This thick and chunky sauce is spicy enough to serve on its own, but much better as a topping for succulent herb-roasted chicken or crispy duck breasts. Any leftovers can be served on toast topped with melting cheese.

PREPARATION TIME: 10 minutes

COOKING TIME: 20 minutes

SERVES: 6

125 g (4 oz) okra

3 tablespoons olive oil

1 onion, finely chopped

2 garlic cloves, thinly sliced

2 bay leaves

400 g (13 oz) can chopped tomatoes

2 teaspoons West Indian pepper sauce or Tabasco sauce

1 teaspoon caster sugar

200 g (7 oz) canned red kidney beans, rinsed and drained

100 ml (3½ fl oz) Vegetable or Chicken Stock (see page 12)

salt

1 Trim the ends from the okra, then cut them across into 1 cm (½ inch) slices. Heat the oil in a large saucepan and fry the okra, onion, garlic and bay leaves gently for 5 minutes until the onion is soft.

2 Add the tomatoes, pepper sauce, sugar, kidney beans and stock. Bring to the boil, then reduce the heat to its lowest setting, cover the pan and cook gently for 15 minutes.

3 Check the seasoning, adding a little salt if necessary, and serve warm.

Ginger, sesame and star anise sauce

Like most Asian-style sauces, this tangy, aromatic one is low in fat and suitable for a healthy, light lunch or supper dish. It enhances poached or pan-fried chicken, duck, pigeon breasts or stir-fries and also goes very well with steamed fish.

PREPARATION TIME: 5 minutes

COOKING TIME: 10 minutes

SERVES: 4

50 g (2 oz) fresh root ginger

2 tablespoons sesame seeds

1 tablespoon vegetable oil

1 tablespoon sesame oil

½ bunch of spring onions, thinly sliced

2 garlic cloves, thinly sliced

100 ml (3½ fl oz) Vegetable or Chicken Stock
(see page 12)

4 tablespoons oyster sauce

2 tablespoons rice wine vinegar

4 whole star anise

1 teaspoon caster sugar

100 g (3½ oz) small oyster mushrooms

1 Peel the ginger and cut half of it into very fine slices. Cut the slices across into fine shreds and place in a small bowl. Grate the remaining ginger. Squeeze the grated ginger over the bowl to extract as much juice as possible. Scrape any juice from the chopping board into the bowl.

2 Heat a small saucepan and gently fry the sesame seeds for 2 minutes until lightly toasted. Remove and set aside.

3 Heat the vegetable and sesame oils in the pan and fry the spring onions and garlic for 1 minute. Add the stock, oyster sauce, vinegar, star anise, sugar, ginger shreds and juice and bring gently to a simmer. Cover with a lid and cook gently for 5 minutes.

4 Add the mushrooms and heat for 1 minute. Serve with the seeds sprinkled over the sauce.

This chapter includes all the delicious sweet sauces that give puddings and desserts a mouthwatering finishing touch. A dark and delicious chocolate sauce is everyone's favourite, lavished over a hot chocolate cake, a pancake stack or a pile of profiteroles. A simple steamed sponge pudding can be utterly transformed as it soaks up the sweet, sticky flavour of a Lemon Butter Sauce or Caramel and Hazelnut Sauce. For those who prefer a lighter finish, there are elegant fruit sauces or an airy Cinnamon Sabayon. Made in minutes and infinitely versatile, these sauces are a pudding lover's dream. Even a pot of yogurt or bowl of ice-cream takes on a whole new image with a sweet and delicious sauce topping.

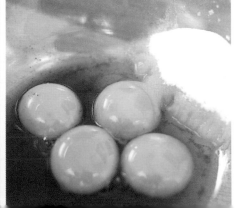

Glossy chocolate sauce

A good chocolate sauce should be smooth and glossy and taste almost like pure melted chocolate. Use a good quality dark chocolate with about 70 per cent cocoa solids to give a rich flavour and plenty of sheen. Take care not to overheat the chocolate or the sauce will develop a grainy texture.

PREPARATION TIME: 5 minutes
COOKING TIME: 2–3 minutes
SERVES: 5–6

125 g (4 oz) caster sugar
125 ml (4 fl oz) water
200 g (7 oz) plain dark chocolate
25 g (1 oz) unsalted butter

1 Put the sugar into a small heavy-based saucepan with the water. Cook over a low heat, stirring constantly with a wooden spoon, until the sugar has completely dissolved.

2 Bring the syrup to the boil and boil for 1 minute, then remove the pan from the heat and leave to cool for 1 minute. Chop the chocolate into pieces and tip them into the pan.

3 Add the butter and leave until the chocolate and butter have melted, stirring frequently, until the sauce is smooth and glossy. If the last of the chocolate doesn't melt completely or you want to serve the sauce warm, return the pan briefly to the lowest heat setting.

Glossy chocolate sauce

Great with: *ice-cream, profiteroles, hot chocolate puddings and poached pears*

Minted white chocolate sauce

Melting chocolate into a mint syrup eliminates any worry of heating it to a solid lump, as is so often the case when using white chocolate. Use a good quality chocolate as cheaper brands have an over-sweet, cloying flavour.

PREPARATION TIME: 5 minutes, plus standing

COOKING TIME: 3 minutes

SERVES: 4

15 g (½ oz) mint leaves

1 tablespoon caster sugar

4 tablespoons water

150 g (5 oz) white chocolate, chopped

150 ml (¼ pint) double cream

1 Pull the mint leaves from the stalks and put them into a small saucepan with the sugar and water. Heat gently until the sugar has dissolved and the mint leaves have wilted. Bring just to the boil. Remove the pan from the heat and leave to stand for 5 minutes, then remove the mint leaves, squeezing out the syrup.

2 Add the chopped chocolate to the syrup and leave for about 2 minutes until melted, stirring frequently until smooth.

3 Add the cream and blend until smooth. Reheat gently if serving warm or transfer to a small jug and leave to cool. The sauce will gradually thicken as it cools, particularly if it is kept in the refrigerator. Serve with poached fruit such as pears or peaches or poured over dark chocolate puddings and soufflés or with ice-cream.

Variations: Use a good quality plain dark chocolate instead of the white for a rich glossy sauce. For a special dessert, the two sauces look stunning swirled together.

Buttery hazelnut syrup

Chunky pieces of toasted hazelnut bathed in a smooth caramel sauce is a delicious combination made using everyday ingredients, perfect for an impromptu pudding.

PREPARATION TIME: 5 minutes

COOKING TIME: 10 minutes

SERVES: 4–5

50 g (2 oz) whole blanched hazelnuts

75 g (3 oz) golden caster sugar

100 ml (3½ fl oz), plus 3 tbsp, water

finely grated rind of 1 small orange

40 g (1½ oz) unsalted butter

1 Chop the nuts into chunky pieces and lightly toast them, either under the grill or in a frying pan.

2 Put the sugar into a small heavy-based saucepan with 100 ml (3½ fl oz) water and heat gently until the sugar dissolves. Bring to the boil and boil rapidly until the syrup has turned to a deep, golden caramel. Immerse the base of the pan in cold water to prevent further cooking.

3 Add 3 tablespoons cold water to the pan with the hazelnuts, orange rind and butter. Return to the heat and cook gently, stirring with a wooden spoon until smooth. Serve warm with pancakes, drop scones, baked bananas or apples.

Butterscotch fudge sauce *Muscovado sugar and evaporated milk give this sauce its distinctive and delicious flavour, great for those who like hot puddings bathed in a sweet, warm creamy puddle. It's especially good with warm banana cake or pudding, thick creamy yogurt or apple pie.*

PREPARATION TIME: 5 minutes

COOKING TIME: 5 minutes

SERVES: 4–6

75 g (3 oz) **unsalted butter**
150 g (5 oz) **light muscovado sugar**
175 g (6 oz) **can evaporated milk**

1 Cut the butter into pieces and put them into a small heavy-based saucepan with the sugar. Heat very gently, stirring with a wooden spoon, until the butter has melted and the sugar dissolved. Bring to the boil and boil for about 2 minutes until the mixture is bubbling and treacly.

2 Remove the pan from the heat. Pour in the evaporated milk and stir gently until evenly combined. Return the pan to the heat, bring the sauce to the boil and cook for 1 minute until smooth and glossy. Pour into a jug and serve hot.

Fresh ginger sauce *Although used mostly in savoury Asian and Indian dishes, fresh ginger tastes extremely good in cakes, desserts and sauces. Its fresh, spicy flavour seeps irresistibly into warm sponges and baked fruits and it's perfect with warm apple, pear or almond tarts.*

PREPARATION TIME: 5 minutes

COOKING TIME: 8 minutes

SERVES: 4–6

50 g (2 oz) **piece of fresh root ginger, peeled**
50 g (2 oz) **golden caster sugar**
150 ml (¼ pint) **apple juice**
2 tablespoons **lime juice**
300 ml (½ pint) **double cream**

1 Grate the ginger and put it into a small heavy-based saucepan, scraping the gratings from the grater and chopping board into the pan. Add the sugar and apple juice and heat gently until the sugar dissolves. Bring to the boil and cook for 3 minutes until turning syrupy.

2 Strain the mixture through a sieve into a clean pan, pressing the pulp in the sieve with the back of a spoon to extract all the juice.

3 Add the lime juice and cream, bring to the boil and boil for 2–3 minutes until slightly thickened. Pour the sauce into a jug and serve warm or leave to cool.

Cinnamon sabayon

Sweet, foamy sabayon can be served as a dessert on its own or, more frequently, as a light and airy sauce. It needs to be made just before serving as it will slowly collapse but you can have all the ingredients measured and waiting, to avoid too much last-minute preparation.

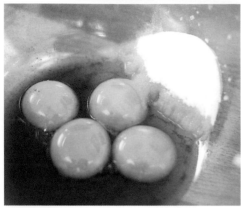

PREPARATION TIME: 5 minutes

COOKING TIME: 10 minutes, plus standing

SERVES: 5–6

¼ **teaspoon ground cinnamon**

4 tablespoons cold water

4 tablespoons coffee liqueur

4 egg yolks

25 g (1 oz) caster sugar

1 Blend the cinnamon with the cold water in a large heatproof bowl. Add the coffee liqueur, egg yolks and caster sugar.

2 Set the bowl over a saucepan of gently simmering water making sure the base of the bowl does not come in contact with the water or the sauce will overheat.

3 Using a balloon whisk or a hand-held electric whisk, beat the ingredients for about 5 minutes until they are light and aerated and the whisk leaves a trail when lifted from the mixture.

4 If you are serving the sauce hot, serve it immediately. If it is to be served cold, remove the bowl from the heat and whisk for a further 2–3 minutes, then leave it to stand for 10 minutes.

Variations: For an orange liqueur sabayon, omit the cinnamon and use Cointreau, Grand Marnier or another orange-flavoured liqueur instead of the coffee liqueur. For a creamier flavour, fold 150 ml (¼ pint) whipping cream, whipped until lightly peaking, into the sauce.

Cinnamon sabayon

Great with: *apple, pear or plum tarts, almond sponges, soft fruit salad or in tall glasses with dessert biscuits*

Mango, passion fruit and rum sauce

Any fruits that can be blended to a thick purée make quick and easy sauces. Choose a ripe and juicy mango and combine with passion fruit and rum to give it extra bite. This sauce is excellent with tropical fruit or vanilla cheesecake, banana cake and ice cream.

PREPARATION TIME: 10 minutes, plus chilling
SERVES: 3–4

1 large mango, chilled
2 passion fruit
juice of ½ orange
2 tablespoons rum

1 Halve the mango either side of the flat stone. Scoop the flesh from the two halves and around the stone into a food processor or blender. Halve the passion fruit and press the pulp through a small strainer to extract the juice.

2 Add the juice to the mango with the orange juice and rum and blend until completely smooth, scraping down the mixture from the sides of the bowl if necessary. Pour into a serving jug and chill until ready to serve.

Slump
When summer fruits are lightly cooked with sugar, they're transformed into a delicious sauce that's as good to eat on its own with a splash of cream as it is as an accompaniment. Serve it with vanilla or soft fruit ice cream, thick yogurt, steamed sponges and crêpes, and stir in a splash of orange liqueur or Kirsch if you like.

PREPARATION TIME: 5 minutes
COOKING TIME: 5 minutes
SERVES: 6

500 g (1 lb) mixed summer fruits, such as strawberries, raspberries, blackberries, redcurrants or blackcurrants
25 g (1 oz) caster sugar

1 Hull the strawberries. If using red- or blackcurrants use the tines of a fork to remove the currants from the stalks.

2 Put all the fruits into a large saucepan with the sugar and a dash of water. Cook very gently for about 5 minutes, stirring frequently, until the fruits are very tender. Serve hot.

Syllabub with lemon and vodka

Syllabub is a frothy, whipped cream dessert that's excellent served on its own with meringues or some buttery dessert biscuits. It can also be served as an accompaniment to summer fruit salad, tarte tatin and other warm fruit tarts, or as a topping for trifle.

PREPARATION TIME: 10 minutes, plus standing

SERVES: 4–6

150 ml (¼ pint) dessert wine

3 tablespoons vodka

juice of 1 large lemon

50 g (2 oz) caster sugar

300 ml (½ pint) double cream

1 Mix together the wine, vodka, lemon juice and sugar, and leave to stand for 10 minutes, stirring frequently to dissolve the sugar.

2 Whip the cream in a mixing bowl until softly peaking using a balloon whisk or a hand-held electric whisk.

3 While whisking, gradually pour the wine mixture into the cream so it remains very softly peaking. Spoon into glasses and serve immediately, or chill until ready to serve.

Brandy butter
Although you can add various flavours to this recipe, such as grated citrus rind or spices, you can't beat a good brandy butter in its simplest form, lightly whipped so it melts readily into the hot Christmas pud. Any leftovers are good on toasted teacakes, pancakes or with baked apples.

PREPARATION TIME: 10 minutes, plus chilling

SERVES: 6–8

125 g (4 oz) unsalted butter, softened

75 g (3 oz) golden icing sugar

4–5 tablespoons brandy

1 Put the butter into a bowl and whisk thoroughly using a balloon whisk or a hand-held electric whisk until smooth and creamy.

2 Add the icing sugar and brandy and whisk again until the sauce is light and creamy. Turn the sauce into a small serving bowl, cover and chill for up to 1 week. Remove the brandy butter from the refrigerator about 30 minutes before serving to let it soften slightly.

Variations: Rum, Drambuie or an orange-flavoured liqueur can be used instead of the brandy.

Red fruit coulis

Two or three summer fruits, blended and strained to a smooth and colourful purée, make a useful sauce for setting off all sorts of summery desserts. Use the coulis to flood the serving plates or drizzle it around the edges. Either way, it will really enhance the presentation.

PREPARATION TIME: 10 minutes, plus cooling
SERVES: 6–8

3 tablespoons caster sugar

about 50 ml (3½ fl oz) boiling water

500 g (1 lb) ripe summer fruits, such as strawberries, raspberries and redcurrants

2–3 teaspoons lemon juice

1 Put the sugar into a small jug and make it up to 50 ml (3½ fl oz) with boiling water. Stir until the sugar dissolves and leave to cool.

2 Remove the redcurrants, if using, from their stalks by running them through the tines of a fork. Place all the fruits in a food processor or blender and blend to a smooth purée, scraping the mixture down from the sides of the bowl if necessary. Blend in the sugar syrup.

3 Pour the sauce into a sieve set over a bowl. Press the purée with the back of a large metal spoon to squeeze out all the juice.

4 Stir in enough lemon juice to make the sauce slightly tangy, then transfer it to a jug. To serve, pour a little coulis onto each serving plate and gently tilt the plate so it is covered in an even layer. Alternatively, use a tablespoon to drizzle the sauce in a ribbon around the edges.

Variations: Replace up to 200 g (7 oz) of the red fruits with blackcurrants, blackberries or mulberries and add 2–3 tablespoons Cassis or an orange liqueur. To make a more autumnal coulis, which is delicious with apple and banana desserts, use only blackberries and double the sugar.

Red fruit coulis

Great with: *chocolate cheesecake, vanilla ice cream, pancakes and fruit tarts*

Coffee bean sauce
Use this smooth coffee syrup to add the finishing touch to a special dessert, spooning it over or around it, whichever looks best. Chocolate soufflé or tart, and chocolate, coffee or vanilla ice cream are all enhanced by this delicious sauce.

PREPARATION TIME: 3 minutes, plus standing

COOKING TIME: 8 minutes

SERVES: 6

250 g (8 oz) golden caster sugar

250 ml (8 fl oz) water

25 g (1 oz) dark roast coffee beans

1 tablespoon lemon juice

1 Put the sugar into a small heavy-based saucepan with the water. Heat gently, stirring, until the sugar has dissolved.

2 Bring the syrup to the boil, then reduce the heat and add the coffee beans and lemon juice. Simmer the syrup gently for 5 minutes. Remove the pan from the heat and leave to stand for 5 minutes.

3 Using a slotted spoon, remove the coffee beans and serve the sauce warm or cold.

Orange cheesecake cream
This recipe can transform the simplest pudding into a special treat. Try spoonfuls on a slice of warm almond or vanilla sponge, with baked or poached fruits, or simply accompanying a plate of freshly cut fruit, particularly juicy melon. For a special dessert, stir in 3 tablespoons orange liqueur, rum or vodka.

PREPARATION TIME: 5 minutes, plus chilling

COOKING TIME: 3 minutes

SERVES: 6

finely grated rind and juice of 1 orange

4 tablespoons coarse or fine cut orange marmalade

250 g (8 oz) mascarpone cheese

150 ml (¼ pint) single cream

1 Put the orange rind and juice in a small heavy-based saucepan with the marmalade and cook over a gentle heat, stirring until the marmalade has melted. Turn the mixture into a bowl and leave to cool for 5 minutes.

2 Add the mascarpone and stir gently until just combined. Stir in the cream.

3 Turn into a serving dish and chill until ready to serve.

Tangy lemon butter sauce

This is an absolutely delicious sauce, rather like a citrusy Crêpe Suzette sauce, only with more lemon giving it a tangier flavour. Ideal for making ahead, simply reheat it and pour over steamed sponge and suet puddings, almond tarts, crêpes or waffles.

PREPARATION TIME: 5 minutes

COOKING TIME: 7 minutes

SERVES: 4

3 lemons

75 g (3 oz) golden caster sugar

juice of 1 orange

50 g (2 oz) unsalted butter

3 tablespoons limoncello or orange liqueur
(optional)

1 Pare the rind carefully from one of the lemons and cut it into fine shreds with a sharp knife. Squeeze the juice from all the lemons.

2 Put the sugar into a heavy-based frying pan with half the lemon juice and the pared rind. Heat gently, stirring, until the sugar has dissolved. Bring to the boil and cook until the syrup starts to turn golden around the edges, about 2–3 minutes.

3 Add the remaining lemon juice, the orange juice and butter to the pan and cook, stirring frequently, until the butter has melted. Stir in the liqueur, if using, and let the sauce bubble for about 2 minutes until it is rich and syrupy. Serve warm.

Crème anglaise

Smooth, creamy and comforting, custard is always a great favourite and well worth the effort of making from scratch. You can vary the proportions of cream to milk depending on personal preference but this recipe, using half cream and half milk, creates a good balance of flavours.

PREPARATION TIME: 10 minutes, plus infusing
COOKING TIME: 10–15 minutes
SERVES: 6

1 vanilla pod, split lengthways
300 ml (½ pint) full cream milk
300 ml (½ pint) single cream
6 egg yolks
25 g (1 oz) caster sugar

1 Put the vanilla pod into a heavy-based saucepan with the milk and cream and bring slowly to the boil. Remove from the heat and leave to infuse for 15 minutes.

2 Whisk together the egg yolks and sugar in a bowl with a balloon whisk until thick and pale. Lift the vanilla pod out of the pan and scrape the seeds into the pan.

3 Pour the milk over the creamed mixture, whisking well. Return the mixture to the cleaned pan and cook over a medium heat, stirring constantly with a wooden spoon, until the sauce thickly coats the back of the spoon. This will take about 5–10 minutes, but don't be tempted to raise the heat or the custard might curdle. Serve warm.

Variations: For a chocolate custard, omit the vanilla and stir 50 g (2 oz) chopped plain dark chocolate into the sauce as soon as it has thickened, stirring until melted. For a coffee custard, omit the vanilla and add 1 tablespoon instant espresso coffee when heating the milk. Two teaspoons of vanilla extract can be used to replace the vanilla pod.

Crème anglaise

Great with: *hot steamed puddings and fruit pies*

Index

Acknowledgments

Photography: © Octopus Publishing Group Ltd / Stephen Conroy

Executive Editor Sarah Ford
Editor Jessica Cowie
Executive Art Editor and Design Geoff Fennell
Production Controller Jo Sim
Food Stylist Joanna Farrow